A Practical Guide to Working with Young Children

Christine Hobart   Jill Frankel

Stanley Thornes (Publishers) Ltd

First published in 1992 by:
Stanley Thornes (Publishers) Ltd
Ellenborough House
Wellington Street
CHELTENHAM GL50 1YD
England

Reprinted 1992
Reprinted 1993

British Library Cataloguing in Publication Data

A catalogue record for this book is available from The British Library.

0–7487–1375–1

Typeset by Tech-Set, Gateshead, Tyne & Wear.
Printed and bound in Great Britain at The Bath Press, Avon.

Contents

Acknowledgements

We would like to thank our colleagues in the Department of Social Services at North London College for their support and encouragement.

A special thank you to Christopher Satterthwaite for taking photographs at the Margaret McMillan Centre, and Ken Garland for his invaluable help and advice.

We would also like to thank the students we have taught over the years, and the training supervisors who ensured their success.

About the authors

Christine Hobart, Cert Ed., RHV, RGN, FWT, is Co-ordinator of NNEB validated courses at North London College. She is an external and internal examiner for the NNEB.

Jill Frankel, MA Child Development, B.Ed., was Course Tutor at the same college. She is an internal examiner for the NNEB.

The authors come from a background of health visiting and nursery teaching, and worked together in Camden before meeting again at North London College. For the past nine years, they have been part of a course team, involved in the development of many innovative courses for the NNEB, including the Camden Training Centre Course for Unemployed Adults, the Orthodox Jewish Certificate in Childcare for the Hassedic community, the three-year part-time Diploma Course and the new Certificate in Playskills.

Introduction

In the experience of the authors, there are no basic guides for childcare students working with children from birth to the age of 7 on how to achieve success in training placements and work experience. Despite preparation by college tutors, the practical work, routines of the placement, and the expectations of supervisors can often prove daunting. In our view, the more knowledge and information that students can obtain, the more likely they are to settle easily into a professional team, to contribute sooner to the work, and to gain skills and competences quickly.

In writing this book, we have deliberately excluded theoretical background information and recommended reading, as we feel this is the terrain of the college tutors. The chapter on Communicating with Young Children was included as communication is seen as a vital element of a student's relationship with the children.

We have emphasised professionalism and equal opportunities as there is little concerning these areas in standard childcare textbooks. We feel very strongly that all childcare workers should have a professional approach, and a key component of this is a clear understanding of equal opportunities policies and their implementation in the workplace.

We have discussed how students might cope with assessment, but have avoided looking at assessment procedures as these will vary from course to course, and are subject to continuous change. In addition, the introduction of National Vocational Qualifications is altering the whole structure of assessment.

Throughout the book, checklists have been included to allow the reader to assess his or her progress regularly. Activities have been suggested in each chapter. In chapters which deal with particular age groups, the activities are often appropriate to other age groups as well.

Although we are associated with two particular childcare courses validated by the NNEB, we have attempted not to use these as models for the book, but to look at the needs of all childcare students, young or mature, full or part-time, male or female. We have deliberately reduced the amount of text and the size of the book to keep it within the price range of students, and to enable them to use it as a handy source of reference when they are in placement.

Christine Hobart and Jill Frankel, 1992

1 So you Want to Work with Young Children?

If you are thinking of a career working with young children, there are several issues you should think about. Many would-be students feel it is enough to like children, to be 'good with kids', but there is a great deal more to childcare than just enjoying being around children.

Check list Have you had experience working with children?

Are you in good health, and will you have the stamina to complete the course?

Do you have literacy skills at a level necessary to undertake the study?

Do you have a range of interests and hobbies?

Do you have the sort of personality that allows you not only to relate well with children, but also to stimulate them to learn, and to enable them to feel secure with you?

Do you feel comfortable working with adults, and are you able to accept constructive criticism?

Experience

It is important to have spent some time with *groups* of children, not just baby-sitting two or three at a time. Young children in large groups are noisy, messy and occasionally quite hard to control. You need to be able to tolerate a high level of noise, enjoy messy activities, show infinite patience, and be firm and consistent.

Health

Are you in good health? Looking after children is a strenuous physical job as well as an intellectually stimulating one. Young children are prone to many minor illnesses, and you will need to build up an immunity to coughs and colds very quickly. If you have recurrent back problems, it would be advisable to seek medical advice before embarking on a childcare career.

Qualifications

Entry requirements for courses in colleges will vary in details such as age, formal qualifications, and entry tests. Some courses will allow you to start training from the age of 16. Those who are more mature and have had more experience of life are particularly welcome. Men and women who represent the ethnic groups within the local community have much to offer.

ACTIVITY

Contact your local college(s) and ask for the prospectus. Look carefully at the range of childcare courses and the entry requirements. Choose the one most suitable for your needs and circumstances.

Interests

Those working with young children need outside interests and hobbies, as these interests can be brought into the placements. A love of music, enjoying reading, skill at craft activities, an understanding of art, an interest in nature and animals: all these experiences can be shared with the children.

Personality

The sort of personality you have will affect the children with whom you are working. Many shy people feel they can relate well with children, whilst having difficulty conversing with adults. You will have to work very closely with many adults; colleagues, other professionals, and parents. Confidence in yourself is the key, whether you have a quiet calm manner, or a lively impetuous nature. A sense of humour is especially important when working with children and with other people in a team.

Disclosure of criminal background

If you have had a brush with the law in the past, you will need to discuss this with the course tutor as soon as you apply. Anyone working with children has to have a possible criminal background checked by the police records department.

Finding out

If you decide on a career working with young children, you will find it very enlightening to talk to childcare workers and to those presently undergoing a course of training. The more knowledge you can gain initially, the better prepared you will be once you start your course.

ACTIVITY

Draw up a profile of yourself using the following headings.

	Strengths	Weaknesses
Health record		
Interests/hobbies		
Personality		
Communication skills: written oral		
Reliability		
Knowledge of different cultures		

2 The First Placement

Preparing yourself

At the start of your course, your tutor will probably give you details of your first placement, with the name of your supervisor, and the organiser/head teacher. In many colleges, there may be a visit to the placement prior to starting full time, and it will be up to you to find the most convenient and quickest route from your home to the placement.

Presenting yourself

First impressions count for a good deal, and if you can show your supervisor right from the start that you are a well-organised and reliable person, you stand a very good chance of success. Arrive a little before the expected time, and seek out the Head/organiser to let him or her know that you are on the premises. Take with you some personal information, such as your past experience with children, other qualifications and interests, and the name of someone to contact should it be necessary in any emergency. Whenever going into a placement you should have with you pens, pencils and a small notebook.

Although an appointment will have been made for you with the placement, the supervisor may be busy with the children when you arrive, so be prepared to sit down with a small group of children and enter quietly into any activity they may be doing, until such time as the supervisor is free. Introduce yourself clearly, and listen carefully to any information which your supervisor gives you. Before leaving the building, check that you will be working with the appropriate age group, and that you have the correct telephone number.

Appearance

Your appearance should be neat, and you must be scrupulously careful with your personal hygiene. Your hair should be tidy, your nails short and well cared-for, your clothing non-restricting, and your shoes flat and comfortable so that you are able to take a full part in the nursery day. Inappropriate clothes would be, for example, high heels and smart clothes that you are afraid of getting dirty. On the other hand, torn or very shabby clothing is equally inappropriate. Jeans are often unacceptable in schools.

The first impression

People often remember their first impression of you, and it is on this that further judgements may be based. If you feel very nervous, try some relaxation exercises, take some deep breaths, and start your visit with a smile on your face and a cheerful and eager expression. Be sensitive to the atmosphere in the room, and aware that supervisors may have many demands on their time and attention.

What to look for during the visit

Now is the time to turn your attention to the children in the room. You will need to know how many children are on the register and how old they are. In cities, there may be children from several cultural backgrounds, and perhaps some who do not speak English at home. Some children may come part time.

Have a look at the building you will be working in. It may be purpose-built, or converted from an old house. The room may be spacious, or rather cramped. The outside play area may have grass, flowers and trees, or it may be a rectangle with a hard surface and no planted area at all.

Check list   ## What you need to ask your supervisor

What time do I need to arrive in the morning?

What time can I expect to leave in the afternoon?

What room will I be working in?

What breaks will I have?

Will I have to pay for any meals?

Is there a booklet about the placement that I can take away and study?

May I have a copy of the equal opportunities policy, and the anti-racist and anti-sexist policy statements?

Are there any policies on discussing a child's progress with parents?

How large is the staff team, and what are the names of the other staff members?

Is it possible for someone to give me a tour of the building?

How many children are there in the room in which I will be working? How many boys and how many girls?

Are the children part time or full time – or are there some of each?

Do any of the children have health needs of which I should be aware?

What are the cultural backgrounds of the children? How many different languages do they speak?

Are there any clothing restrictions for staff?

Check list   **What you will need before you leave**

The telephone number of the placement.

The name of the Head/organiser.

The name of the supervisor.

ACTIVITY

Using the checklist, describe your placement fully. When next in college, sit down with other students in your group and compare notes.

The local environment

When you leave the placement take some time walking round the local area. See what sort of homes most of the children live in. They might be living in blocks of flats or in houses with gardens. There may be shops and markets nearby. The placement might be rather isolated, or there could be parks and a community centre and easy access to public transport. You will find that the mix of the children, the suitability of the building, and the pleasantness or otherwise of the environment in which the children live may well have a bearing on their behaviour and their ability to concentrate. A cultural mix of children will lead to richer experiences. A large airy room and a beautiful garden with grass and trees will induce a calm atmosphere among staff and children. An interesting and exciting environment will lend itself to many outings and visits within the community.

ACTIVITY

1 After your visit, walk around the area and make short notes on housing, transport and community facilities for children, such as clinics, swimming pools and libraries. There may be parks, zoos, clubs, farms, and open wild areas.

2 Visit the nearest library, and see if there is a section for children's books. Enquire if you will be able to borrow these for the children whilst working in your placement. Look at the community information board. There may be a great deal more happening in the area than you have discovered.

Settling in

Having started your placement, you will find it easier to develop good relationships with the staff team if you take as full a part as possible in all activities, demonstrating enthusiasm and a willingness to learn. Placements expect their students to undertake any appropriate task asked of them, including occasional involvement in activities outside the placement hours.

Working with the team

After a week or two, you will be ready to show initiative, seeing tasks that need to be done without having to be directed, contributing your own ideas for activities, and being sensitive to the needs of the placement and of the children. You will find yourself making suggestions at regular team meetings, drawing on your observations of the children and your own interests and perceptions.

Many students find it useful to keep a diary to make a note of questions they need to ask, and activities in which they have participated. Arrange a time each week with your supervisor to discuss your progress and the difficulties you may have encountered. Ask your supervisor to read and sign your observations. You will need to find out your role in the placement programme for the next time you are there.

Taking part in the social life of the placement is very important. Try to arrange to use the staff room at break times, so that the staff can see that you think of yourself as one of them. You may find it intimidating at first, but with a little effort on your part you will soon relax and become a full member of the team.

Being reliable

You should always be punctual, arriving at least half an hour before the children. If ever you might be unavoidably late, make sure you telephone and let the placement know. If you should be ill, and unable to attend the placement, you must telephone as soon as possible, and keep in touch on a daily basis, so that they will know when to expect you back.

As you gain in confidence, you will make good and lasting relationships with children and colleagues, and you are likely to thoroughly enjoy your time in your placement.

Check list

After 12 days in the placement

Are you arriving at the expected time?

Have you stayed after hours, either to attend a meeting or to discuss children or activities?

Have you attended every day?

Have you telephoned if you have been absent or late?

Do you know the names and ages of all the children?

Do the children know your name?

Are the children pleased to see you when you return after a break?

Do you know the names and the roles of all the staff team?

Have you used the staff room?

Have you managed to arrange a time to see your supervisor every week, to discuss your progress?

Have you enjoyed being with the children, looking forward to every day?

Do you have a clear understanding of what is expected of you in the placement?

3 Communicating with Young Children

Children learn about the world around them through the senses: touch, sight, hearing, smell and taste. The newborn baby will very quickly recognise the mother by the use of all the senses. Because of this, the way a stranger handles a baby immediately communicates either a feeling of security or of threat. Someone who wishes to work with young children needs to be responsive, warm and caring, and this will show in the way they hold a baby or dress a toddler.

Good practice | **When handling young children**

1 Approach children calmly and quietly, using your voice to encourage co-operation.

2   Make eye contact with children before attempting to pick them up.

3   Sit on the floor with young children; if you tower over them they might feel threatened.

4   Changing a baby's napkin, brushing a child's hair, and helping a child to use the lavatory are all intimate activities, and preferably should only be carried out once a good relationship has been established.

5   Children's need to be cuddled should be met, although some schools might frown on physical contact with older children. A child will feel safe and secure if his or her needs are met swiftly and responsively. Refusing to pick up and cuddle a child who obviously wants you to is not only bad practice but can be harmful to the development of the child.

6   Be aware of the child's non-verbal communication.

ACTIVITY

Sit with a friend and brush his or her hair, first roughly, not looking, as if your thoughts are elsewhere. Then repeat gently. Change places with your friend, and then discuss how you both felt.

Speech

An important way of communicating with children is through the use of spoken language. Very few children have any memories of the time before they were two years old, as this is the age when they start to put thoughts into words.

It has become apparent that the attainment of children in schools is highly influenced by their mastery of language. Children's ability to speak and understand 'book language' is the key achievement in all areas of the school curriculum. The sooner that children become fluent in expressive language (speech) and develop their comprehension (understanding), the better they get on in school and with their peer group.

It has also been shown that, whilst most language is learnt in the home, pre-school provision of any sort enriches and extends children's language. Children will develop language skills by talking both with sensitive and understanding adults and with other children. It is obviously most important for carers of the under-fives to choose their language carefully, so as to capitalise on this most sensitive age for acquiring language.

Children who use a different language at home to that of the school will have some initial difficulty in understanding all that goes on around them. However, to be fluent in two languages is a great advantage in later life, as it will lead to the easier learning of third and fourth languages. Children find it natural to learn a second language in a nursery with good practice, and it is unnecessary to make special provision for them to learn English. Young children do need an opportunity to use their heritage language. This should be encouraged. A child whose knowledge of English is only just emerging is not delayed in other areas of development, and must not be treated as such.

Good practice

When speaking to young children

1   Try not to ask children 'closed' questions, where you know the answer (e.g. 'What colour are your shoes?'). Depending on the age of the child, he or she will either think you are stupid or else will feel that he or she is being tested.

2   Try not to ask children questions which require just one word as an answer (e.g. 'Do you like apples?'). This sort of question does not extend the children's speech, and the talk is dominated by the adult.

3   Some of the activities in the nursery lend themselves to adults and children sitting down together, and these times are excellent for making children feel comfortable and relaxed, so that a conversation can take place. Sitting round the dough or clay table is one such situation; dinner time is another.

4   If you want children to carry out a task you must make sure that you explain it simply and clearly. Asking a child if he or she would like to help you clear up might justify the answer 'no'; the child is not necessarily being defiant, but will respond much better if you just tell him or her politely to do it.

5   Never ask children to do several things at once. For example, 'Before you go outside, I would like everyone to have had his or her snack or drink. Remember to put your coats on; it is cold today. Those of you with hats and gloves, make sure you put them on in the classroom, before you go outside. And tidy up the room first, I don't want anyone going out before the whole classroom is spick and span.' Many children, when they heard the magic invitation to go outside, would cease listening to the rest of the instructions, and get into trouble for not listening to what is being said.

6   Give children time to work out what they want to say. Young children are not such experienced conversationalists as adults, and need time to respond. Do not try to guess what they want to say, giving them the words. Be prepared to really listen to children, as much more can be learnt by this approach than by dominating the conversation yourself.

7   Build good relationships with those children who do not speak to you straight away. When they trust you sufficiently, they will speak to you. There are often children in the class who are comfortable speaking only to one other child, or to one adult. Respect this, and wait for the child to know you sufficiently well to speak to you.

8   Reading books and telling simple stories to one or two children at a time not only helps in building trusting relationships, but also allows children to hear new words and extend their vocabulary.

9   Talking to children whilst engaged in a play activity with them helps to widen their vocabulary.

10   Try to speak softly, calmly and clearly to children. Obviously you would never shout, but unfortunately some people have loud and strident voices. If you are told to speak more quietly, or to calm down, take this as constructive criticism, and listen to yourself on a tape recorder. You might be surprised at how you sound!

11   Never correct a young child's speech. Grammatical errors are normal for 3 and 4 year-olds, and will correct themselves as the child develops. A variety of different dialects may be used, and different dialects are there for us all to enjoy. No dialect should be considered the 'right' one. It is, however, important that speech can be understood. If a child has difficulty in being understood outside the family, specialist help may be necessary, and you will learn all about this in your work at college.

12   If a child asks you a question to which you do not know the answer, be honest enough to say so, and discuss ways of discovering the answer together.

13   Remember to use music and rhymes with children. Bilingual children in particular often feel more relaxed singing in their second language than speaking it.

14   Try to ignore swearing, and make sure you never use 'bad language' yourself. Children give up swearing if they get no reaction.

ACTIVITY

Tape yourself reading a story to a small group of children. Allow time for questions and discussion, and don't worry if interruptions occur. Leave the book with the cassette and the tape recorder in the book corner. The children will be able to follow the story for themselves.

It will take time for you to be automatically sensitive to your language and body contact with children, and you may even find trained staff slipping up occasionally. As time goes by, and you experience how children can be helped to acquire and develop language and other communication skills, you will be able to devise your own activities and ideas to help children with difficulties in communication and language delay. You will also begin to extend the skills of children who are already articulate and confident.

Be aware that it is easier and more rewarding to some people to converse with children who are already very fluent. There is also a risk of equating fluency in speech with high intelligence, and yet those who are slower to respond may well be thinking more deeply. Ensure that you hold a conversation and communicate with as many children as possible during the day.

ACTIVITY

You must discuss this assignment with your training supervisor first, and ask for advice and permission to tape a conversation with a child who enjoys talking to adults. Your supervisor may feel it necessary to gain the permission of the child's parent or carer first. Collect some toys such as model animals, cars or play people. Then invite the child to sit with you in a quiet corner of the room. Talk with the child about the toys, and see how you can encourage the child to speak. When you play your tape back later:

(a) See how much of the speech is yours and how much is the child's. Usually, adults dominate the conversation without meaning to.

(b) Now look at the quality of the speech. How many open questions did you ask, requiring more from the child than a one-word answer? How many closed questions did you ask, allowing the child to simply answer 'yes' or 'no'? Did the child ask any questions, or initiate any ideas?

If you feel that you might do better if you try again, ask permission to do so. It is quite a difficult skill to listen and give the child time to talk, rather than fill in silences with your own chatter!

Check list *Have you:* spoken to all the children in the placement every day?

spent at least ten minutes with a child who is normally reluctant to talk?

read a story to one child?

read a story to a small group of children?

told a story to one or more children?

made sure that you have spoken in a soft, clear voice?

spoken clearly when you have asked children to perform tasks?

sung songs with the children?

taught the children a new rhyme?

taken time to discuss displays or posters with the children?

4 Succeeding in a Placement

Professionalism

To act professionally in your placement, you must recognise your responsibility to respect the rights of the people with whom you work. This is particularly important for those working with young children, as the children are often unable to communicate their needs adequately.

Reaching this professional state is not something that happens overnight; it is a gradual process. With the help of tutors and supervisors you should regularly assess your knowledge, skills, behaviour and attitudes. You will receive support and encouragement from them.

The professional working with young children will have made progress in three areas: knowledge, behaviour and attitudes.

Knowledge

During your course, both in college and in placement, you will be gaining knowledge; that is, learning through theory and observation the aesthetic, moral, intellectual, physical, emotional, social, and language development of children, which will make you sensitive to their needs and so enable you to develop good standards of practice.

Such knowledge plays an important part in preventative work, for example identifying children who are at risk of abuse and in need of protection. You will need to know the procedure for making a referral for specialist help to ensure the safety of these children. Although you may not be directly involved as a student, your supervisor will explain the procedures to you.

As you grow in knowledge you will be better able to understand children in your care, and to interpret records and observations so that you spot problems and ensure that the child receives the necessary help and support.

You will never come to the end of what you can learn about looking after children. A good indicator of a professional person is the willingness to be updated regularly after qualifying by attending courses and reading professional journals. The professional will always be ready to question and challenge in a thoughtful and constructive way. This will include a constant re-evaluation in relation to children's rights, childcare policies, and new education initiatives.

Behaviour

During your placement, your motivation, enthusiasm and commitment will be continually assessed. You should show a positive attitude towards your work becoming aware of your role and responsibilities, and reaching an understanding of what you can and cannot do in the placement.

Good behaviour covers a wide variety of different practises, which we shall look at one by one.

Attendance and punctuality

It is essential to attend college and placement regularly, and to be punctual. If you are unable to attend, or are unavoidably delayed, contact the placement so that they can replan the day. Keep them informed so that they know when to expect your return. You are surplus to staffing requirements as a student, but you will still be seen as a valuable member of the team.

Communication

You will be using three methods of communication: writing, speaking and using body language.

You will need to keep written records, make written observations and write reports.

The clarity of your speech and the ways in which you talk to children, parents and other professional people will show them that you are a caring, knowledgeable and sensitive person. You should be able to state your views and ideas clearly and concisely.

Your body language should convey that you are interested and motivated. Shrugging your shoulders and sulking is no substitute for expressing your point of view over a disagreement calmly and clearly. Maintaining eye contact with children and adults will help foster good relationships.

Teamwork

Whatever the size of the professional team you are working in, you will have to share your knowledge, opinions, and observations in a positive way, whilst valuing the knowledge and expertise of all the team members. The ability to accept and act upon constructive criticism forms part of the student's professional development, and even when you are a qualified childcare worker you will constantly need to look at your practice with others in the team, and be able to offer and accept suggestions for improvement.

Responsibility

The well-being and safety of the children in your care has to be your main concern, and at no time should you behave in a way that might jeopardise this.

No one is perfect in all respects, so understand and acknowledge your limitations. Do not feel forced to take on responsibilities when you do not think that you have had the necessary knowledge and training to carry them out successfully. If, for example, you are asked to look after children on an outing, and feel unprepared for this, discuss it with your supervisor. If you should object on religious or ethical grounds when asked to undertake a task in the placement, you must discuss this in an open way with your tutor and your supervisor. A common example of this is the celebration of some festivals, such as Christmas, to which some religious sects object.

Confidentiality

The staff at your placement will be aware of much confidential information concerning the children and their families. The amount of information disclosed to you will depend on what is necessary to meet the needs of the child, help you to function within the team and to acquire a deeper insight into working with families. All information that you receive, either written or verbal, is strictly confidential. You should never share it with your family and friends. Even your college tutors will not want you to reveal the identities of the children that you observe in your placement.

Talking to parents and children

If parents or carers want to confide in you, remind them that you are still a student; it may be more appropriate for them to discuss the problem with your supervisor or another member of staff. If they wish to talk only to you, ask their permission to confide the information to the supervisor. If children confide in you, you must treat such confidences seriously, and may well need to talk to your supervisor.

ACTIVITY

With a group of friends, discuss how you would cope with a gossiping parent. Would you tell your supervisor the gossip? (It might be of benefit to the family being discussed.) If something potentially serious is being talked about among the parents, such as abuse, should you keep quiet or pass it on to your supervisor, to your college tutor, or to anyone else?

Attachment

Be wary of allowing children to become too attached to you. It is very flattering to have young children clinging to you, but remember that you are only in placement for short periods of time, and cannot provide the continual comfort and care that is sometimes needed.

Opinions

If you have strong religious or political views, the placement is not the place to push them. You may wish to raise some issues in the staffroom or at college, but this would be inappropriate in front of children and their parents.

Attitudes

It will be expected in all your placements that you show awareness of and sympathise with the needs of children, parents and team members, regardless of race, class, culture, religion, disability, gender or age, both individually and in groups. Never show favouritism or special treatment towards some children in preference to others, but always show respect and interest in the customs, values and beliefs of all the children with whom you are involved. This will help you to provide children with positive images of themselves and each other. Make it clear that you will not take part in gossip about children or their families.

Check list Look at the checklist on page 9 again, and ask yourself the same questions now.

Have you made progress?

Assessment in placement

On most courses you are continuously assessed both in college and in placement on your ability to understand academic work and to put your theory into practice. Although this sounds intimidating, as you develop new skills and become competent, success will be self-reinforcing and will give you confidence. You will begin to develop job satisfaction. Assessment also helps you to be sure that you have chosen the right career.

The training placements are chosen by the colleges as suitable work models for students because they offer good practice in caring for and educating children from 0–7 years. For this reason, it is your supervisor who will be responsible for assessing your progress, not only in your practical skills, but in your growing awareness of what it means to be a professional team member.

Assessment in National Vocational Qualifications (NVQs)

NVQs are competence-based qualifications – assessment focuses on performance, practical skills, and how competently tasks are carried out. We will be seeing more and more assessment being carried out in the workplace. Training courses will help students to gain the knowledge and the understanding they need to perform practical tasks satisfactorily.

Visits by your College Tutor

It is one of the responsibilities of your college tutor to visit you in your placement on a regular basis, by previous arrangement with your supervisor. The main reason for your tutor visiting is to discuss with you and your supervisor how you are progressing in the placement. You may wish to raise any problems you are having with your tutor first, and he or she will help you to think about how you can communicate this to your supervisor during the visit. This is part of your learning, as when qualified you will have to discuss difficulties with colleagues and attempt to resolve problems in a positive professional manner.

Often the use of a checklist aids a three-way discussion between a student, a tutor and a supervisor by making sure that all good points are highlighted, whilst allowing any area of concern to be expressed.

If problems are identified and discussed openly, you should be able to voice your point of view, and at the same time be prepared to accept fair, constructive criticism. At the end of the discussion it should be clear what you need to put right any problems and make progress. For example, a student who is constantly late will need either to get up earlier, or to review the route being taken to the placement. Another example would be that a student who finds it difficult to read a story to a group of children needs to be given the chance to start with two or three children only, and to gradually build up to a larger group.

ACTIVITY

Use the chart on p. 22 to assess yourself. How would you complete it? Do you think your tutor would complete it in the same way?

	Poor	Impro-ving	Satis-factory	Good	Very good	N/A
Relationships						
With children						
With staff/colleagues						
With parents						
Ability with children						
Initiative in use of play materials						
Preparation of activities						
Appropriateness of language						
Use of books; storytelling						
Music						
Awareness of children's needs						
Physical						
Social						
Emotional						
Cognitive						
Observation skills						
The placement environment						
Taking part in extra-curricular activities						
Awareness of inside and outside the placement						
Willingness to do chores						
Professionalism						
Attendance						
Punctuality						
Attending staff/team meetings						
Always showing a positive approach						
Ability to take and act on criticism						
Personal appearance						
Work presented on time						

Any other comments:

Satisfactory/unsatisfactory

Signed _____   Supervisor

_____ Student _____ Tutor

Date _____

Example of a chart used by a college tutor when visiting students

Reports

As you finish your time in each placement, your supervisor will be asked to write a report. It is good practice for you to see all your reports, and have the opportunity to discuss them with the supervisor. In general, reports will highlight your strengths and successes, but will also point out areas where progress should be made.

Your supervisor will not expect perfect practice as you are in the process of training, and you must try not to feel threatened or distressed if your report is less flattering than you expected. Make sure you discuss any point you feel unhappy about with your supervisor. Training will not only allow you to gain knowledge and skills, but will be a period of personal growth and development. The supervisor who indicates the good points and neglects to tell you where you might make progress is not helping you to develop all areas of your work.

Your performance in placement will show you whether you have chosen the right career. If the academic work is a struggle but the placement a joy, in the end you are likely to succeed as you will be highly motivated to work very hard. If you find working with the children difficult and often boring you will come to the conclusion yourself that you have made a wrong career choice, and your tutors will guide you on to a more suitable course. Most students will enjoy both the practice and the theory, understanding the need for knowledge to perfect their practical skills.

ACTIVITY

At the end of your time in placement, draw up a list of a) the areas in which you have made progress and b) the areas you feel need to be further improved.

5 Equal Opportunities

Why are equal opportunities important?

A person with a professional attitude needs to recognise that no member of society should be discriminated against because of his or her race, gender, class, culture, age, religion, disability, or sexual orientation. This is especially important for those people working with young children, as the younger you are, the harder it is to confront prejudice. Children need to feel confident about themselves, and to be sure that they are valued. If children are not cared for with a commitment to equal opportunities they may develop negative feelings about themselves which would lead to a lack of self-esteem, and inhibit their development.

We are all products of our environment and heredity. The way we have been treated by our families and by society will have a bearing on how we see others. In spite of legislation against racial and gender discrimination, many people still experience negative and hurtful attitudes.

In your placement you may meet children from different backgrounds and cultures, with many different views of the world, possibly speaking different languages. There may be anti-racist and anti-sexist policies available for you to read.

The need of children with disabilities to have access to equal opportunities is slowly being recognised and addressed. This is starting to be reflected in the recruitment of some students with disabilities on childcare courses.

Some areas of discrimination have been scarcely recognised in the context of childcare. Firstly, few colleges have given much thought to sexual orientation. Secondly, mature students have found difficulty in the past in gaining access to some courses. However, more colleges are now aware of the needs of older people, and the richness of experience they can bring to the courses and to the children.

Gender

Male students

Most childcare courses have difficulty in recruiting men, particularly young men, who might have problems in overcoming the prejudice and negative remarks of their friends. Once on the course, men are appreciated

for the views they can add to group discussion. Placements are most welcoming to men, as some children who are without a male role model at home particularly enjoy the company of a male student. Children coming from homes which have suffered from male violence can see that there are men who are capable of sensitivity and caring.

Gender stereotyping

It is important that you offer all the activities available to all the children. You might find that some parents and some people you are working with still expect to see the girls in the home corner and the boys using the large bricks. If this happens, opportunities are being limited, and the young children are learning limited expectations of gender roles. There is no reason why boys should not grow up to be nurses and girls to be engineers. Attitudes are learnt very young, in the home, from the media and from school influences, and this is all the more reason why the placement should challenge stereotypes. The pressure later on in life for children to conform to certain behaviour is very strong, and it is most important that the children experience equal opportunities in their play at the youngest age. If the boys dominate the outside play and in particular the wheeled toys such as bicycles, they will inhibit the girls from gaining experience in spatial awareness, which may later affect their ability to be mathematicians. The boys need access to the home corner, so that they can play out some of the caring roles they may not be allowed to express at home.

ACTIVITY

With your supervisor's permission, send the girls outside to use the wheeled toys, while the boys have access to the home corner undisturbed.

Friendships

Whatever the policies of the placement are, children are well aware of their own gender, and most 4 year-old boys will play together in groups, while girls of this age will usually choose another girl as 'best friend' and play mainly with her. You should not seek to split up these alliances, but occasionaly it is helpful to encourage the children towards activities they might not choose themselves.

Adults as role models

You and the staff in the placement will be seen as role models by the children. If you are a female student, you must make sure you participate in all the activities, particularly in outside play such as ball games and assault courses, big block construction and woodwork. The male student should be able to join in with confidence in the caring roles in the home corner, cooking, dressing up, and having quiet moments on a one-to-one basis with a child. Look with a critical eye at the nursery environment. The pictures on the wall and in the book corner should show women and men in a variety of roles, such as female doctors and male nurses. The text in the books should express a wide variety of settings and roles for both sexes.

ACTIVITY

Collect some photographs or pictures to use in the placement to challenge stereotypical roles, such as pictures of women pilots.

Good practice

1   Present positive images of all people, especially in the book corner.

2   Be aware of yourself as a good role model.

3   Challenge stereotypes, for example assuming the girls will dress up as nurses and the boys as doctors.

4   Ask all children to participate in all areas of placement life, including moving equipment and doing domestic tasks.

5   Allow boys to cry and express their feelings. Do not expect boys to be 'braver' than girls. Most children enjoy cuddles.

6   Never use gender to divide the children into groups.

7   Look at the expectations you have of children. A boy can comfort a distressed child just as well as a girl. Disagreements leading to fighting are as unacceptable in boys as in girls.

8   If you identify sex discrimination in the use of equipment, establish times to give the other gender a chance to use it.

9   Encourage all children to be assertive and stand up for themselves.

Communication

In some placements, boys seem to monopolise the attention of the adults with rough and noisy play, or demanding adult time. You need to be aware of this, and make sure you value the contribution of both boys and girls. Watch your use of language with the children. Make sure that you sometimes comment on how smart a boy might look, and how well a girl has planned a building with the large blocks.

As you gain in experience and confidence, you will be able to deal calmly with parents' queries about all the children having access to all the activities. You will be helping the placement to display and explain the work of children in workshops and at open evenings. By watching your supervisor working with the parents you will gradually acquire the skills needed to communicate with parents and carers in a positive manner.

Race

We live in a multiracial society, and your course and placements may reflect this, recruiting students and welcoming children from many different ethnic groups. If you are a student in a college which does not provide this stimulating and enriching experience, it is even more important that you fully understand the issues around the provision of a multicultural environment and be sensitive to anti-racist policies. A young white student taking a course in an exclusively young white environment in a quiet rural area needs to be aware of and responsive to the rest of society. In areas where students are working solely with white children, there is a responsibility to bring to them the richness of the multiracial world.

What is racism?

Racism manifests itself in various ways:

- Racism supports the idea of one superior race or culture.
- Racism prevents people fulfilling their own potential because of their race.
- Racism creates a hostile atmosphere for people of different ethnic groups, and in this atmosphere learning cannot take place.

Challenging racism

As a student, you will be expected to confront and challenge racism. This could be in the form of a physical assault. It may be in the form of a 'joke', or an insult directed towards an individual. There could be provocative behaviour, such as wearing badges or insignia, or bringing into college offensive literature such as racist magazines, comics or leaflets. It may be in the attitudes of other staff in your placement. Some racism is institutionalised and thoughtless, such as not giving heed to the dietary customs of some groups, and using developmental norms and percentile charts developed for the indigenous white population.

Anti-racist policies

Many placements will have an anti-racist policy spelt out, and you should have access to this. Whatever the policy in your placement, you should make yourself familiar with it. Many students find it difficult to confront racism at first, whether from adults or from children, and may need to discuss strategies for dealing with this issue with their supervisor and college tutors.

Knowledge of many cultures

Children need to have a good understanding of other races, and in the placement many cultures should be reflected. The book corner should have a good selection of books, some of them in other languages. All should have positive images of people and children from all over the world. The home corner should reflect as many different homes as possible. The use of the household equipment from different cultures must be understood by staff and students. The undertaking of home visits by many nurseries would help foster this understanding. Dressing-up clothes from many countries should be included. Music and musical instruments from all over the world also enrich the children's experience. Listening in a positive manner to the children describing their experiences helps staff to become more sensitive. Involving parents in reading to the children, making music with them, cooking different foods, all helps the children realise how much they are valued. Many placements will celebrate a variety of different festivals. This shows appreciation of the various cultures, but the festivals must be prepared and celebrated correctly, with the guidance and expertise of the parents of the children involved, and must be relevant to the needs and the ages of the children.

ACTIVITY

1 Cook a dish with the children using a staple food, such as rice, lentils or maize.

2 Look at the books in your local children's library. Do you think any of them are racist? Why? Name three books you would be happy to use in your placement.

3 If your placement's anti-racist policy is available, bring a copy to your college. Discuss it in the group.

Good practice

1   Present positive images of different races in the room, in particular in the book corner and the home corner.

2   Present yourself as a good anti-racist role model.

3   Acknowledge what you do not know, and be prepared to ask for help and advice.

4   Confront racist remarks, whether from children or from adults, whether directed against yourself or others.

5   Answer children's questions about race and culture honestly, with explanations appropriate to the child's age.

6   Make sure you pronounce and spell all the children's names correctly and understand the naming systems of different cultures and religions. For example, 'Begum' is a female title often assumed to be a family's surname.

7   Make sure you know and pronounce correctly the names of the garments the children wear, and those they use for dressing up.

8   Understand the differing skin and hair care needs of all the children.

9   Encourage children to have positive feelings about their skin colour.

10   Discussion during activities involving painting pictures of themselves helps children to know and appreciate what colouur skin they have.

11   Continually evaluate equipment and books with regard to racism. Dolls, jigsaw puzzles, music and so on should reflect many cultures.

12   Make sure there is a varied menu which will appeal to all children in the nursery, and which will introduce them to a more interesting diet.

13   Encourage all parents to participate in the life of the placement.

14   If you have parents who do not have English as a first language, make sure that all information is given clearly enough for all the parents to understand. An interpreter may be necessary in some placements.

Religion

In college and in your placement you will probably come across many different beliefs and religions. Tolerance, acceptance, and a willingness to learn from others is essential, so that you can develop awareness and sensitivity to the needs of children in your care.

Knowledge of different religious customs and festivals is important to those working with young children. As a student, you should make yourself aware of the various religions that the families may have. Children will not necessarily be able to give you details concerning beliefs, diet, dress and festivals. It is far wiser to involve the parents and community leaders. All religions have many facets, and some believers keep strictly to the orthodox practices, while others of the same faith adopt a more relaxed approach. Some families who see themselves as Christians may only use the Church for christenings, weddings and funerals, rarely going to services at other times. Other devout Christians may attend church every week, and see Sunday as a day of rest and prayer.

ACTIVITY

1 Find out what major religious festivals your placement celebrates during the year. Are there any others?

2 Find out from your supervisor what religions are represented in the placement. What differences might there be in dress, diet, holy days and celebrations?

Whilst attempting to meet the needs of all religions, it is important to remember that some children (and adults) will come from an atheist background. They should not feel excluded or unable to identify with their carers. Whatever religious celebrations are taking place, there should be an emphasis on humanitarianism and caring for others.

1 Make sure that the children have a varied and adequate diet, whilst obeying the dietary laws of their religion.

2 If modest dress is a requirement of the religion, do not insist that the child undresses for games, swimming or physical education.

3 An understanding of the festivals celebrated in the placement is important, and the families should always be consulted.

4 An insult directed towards any religion should be challenged in the same way as you would deal with racism.

Class

On your course, you will learn about the class structures of many different societies as part of Social Studies, and this knowledge will relate to your Health and Education Studies. The United Kingdom is a particularly class-ridden society, and this needs to be acknowledged. There is no legislation to prevent discrimination on grounds of class. It is recognised that children from higher income groups have easier access to higher education.

Social disadvantage

In the placement, you may be working with children from many different backgrounds. Children from all classes have the potential to be equally intelligent, but a very deprived home life can have an effect on all areas of development.

You may find you are meeting children with very different backgrounds from your own for the first time, and working with socially deprived children may arouse distress and anger that a wealthy country such as ours, still has families living below the poverty line. Some placements will try to redress this balance by offering intervention programmes to these children. Working with very wealthy families can also be upsetting, if the children seem to have many different carers employed to look after them and are pushed academically beyond reasonable expectations.

Children's rights

All children, regardless of their background, need and have the right to:

● Physical care, ensuring safety, good health and nutrition

- Emotional care, encompassing warm caring constant relationships
- Intellectual stimulation, including education through play to develop language and cognitive skills to their full potential
- Social relationships, developing friendships, mixing with other children and adults from many different backgrounds, and learning to value people for what they are.

1   Be aware of current welfare benefits and sources of help in the community, such as the primary health care team, and social services.

2   Show sensitivity to, and awareness of, everyone's needs at all times.

3   Involve ALL the parents/carers in the placement in activities and outings.

4   Be aware of the financial pressures on some parents. Do not suggest the child may need new equipment or clothing, even if you think it is necessary.

5   When planning outings, try to go to some places which are free occasionally, such as to the park for a picnic. A small sum of money can be collected each week to pay for a more expensive visit.

6   Have patience with those parents/carers who place too much emphasis on one aspect of development, carefully explaining the all-round needs of the child, and the need to value children for what they are, not what you wish them to be.

7   Develop your role as a health educator. Show by your example the importance of a healthy, nutritious diet, the prevention of infection by scrupulous hygiene, and an awareness of preventative health care.

Age

At college, you may find yourself in a group of young students who have just left school, students with children and family responsibilities, and mature students who have decided they wish to work with children as a second career.

Helping each other

Young students will gain a great deal from the experience of older students. Sometimes a young student with personal problems might find it easier to confide in an older student in the group than in a parent or a tutor. The experiences that parents are having with their own children will help students to understand the rights and responsibilities of all parents.

Sometimes, mature students find study skills difficult at first, and may lack confidence in organising their work and in writing essays. This is where students who have just left school can be of help, not in doing the work itself, but in giving support which will lead to confidence.

All students need to value each other, irrespective of age, and appreciate the perspectives that different generations bring to the work.

In the placement

You may find you relate more easily to younger or to older children. This is perfectly natural, but a professional person will spend equal time with all age groups. When you qualify, you can choose the age group with which you wish to work.

As a mature student, you might find your training supervisor is young enough to be your son or daughter. You must value the qualification which you in turn will receive one day, and be prepared to take constructive criticism. This might be quite difficult to do, and needs tact on all sides, as the supervisor might be finding it hard to give advice to an older person.

As a young student, perhaps finding it hard to accept criticism even from your own parents, you will learn to enjoy the company of an older supervisor, valuing and respecting his or her advice, providing the supervisor realises that you are not a child, but a student, and as such a valuable member of the team.

Good practice

1 Value your peers for what they are, and do not classify people by age.

2 Learn from the experiences offered by your supervisor, whether older or younger than yourself.

3 Give of your best to all children of all ages.

4 Respect adults and children for what they are, regardless of age.

Sexual orientation

You may meet colleagues and parents who are in homosexual relationships, and so you need to have considered the subject of sexual orientation, and how it will affect your work. In the placement it is important to promote positive self-images in children from all family backgrounds, and to encourage caring attitudes, helping the children to understand that people choose different people to be special to them. They will learn to value the choices made by the people who look after them, and to appreciate the range of choices open to them at a later date. Children from all families will see that their home circumstances are valued as highly as others.

Good practice

1   Provide a general atmosphere in which a diversity of close relationships, family backgrounds, and different types of households are valued.

2   Challenge offensive remarks or slang terms used by children or adults.

3   Allow children to use the home corner in a way that reflects their own experiences.

Disability

If you have a student with a disability in your group at college, you will be able to learn at first hand that the emphasis should be on the person, and not on the special need. With some people, the disability might be obvious, but it might take you a little while to discover that your new friend has dyslexia. If you have a special need or disability, sharing your experiences with the group at a time when you feel safe and comfortable will be helpful to them as well as to yourself.

Later in this book, you will find a chapter about working with children in special schools, but you will find children with special needs in all your placements. Such needs are not always physical, but may be emotional, social, intellectual or language needs.

Good practice

1   Think of the person, not the disability. People in wheelchairs are not necessarily deaf!

2   Inform yourself as fully as possible about the cause of the disability, and how you might help the person.

3   There should be positive images of successful disabled people and children in the placement, in posters and books.

4   Discuss the progress of the child with parents and carers, in an open and relaxed manner.

6 Observation Skills and Techniques

Why do observations?

Observing children is an important part of childcare work. Watching children carefully and objectively is a difficult skill to learn. If ten people witness a traffic accident, ten different descriptions will be given to the police. You will need to decide what it is you want to observe, discuss with the supervisor the aim of the observation, and then sit quietly in a corner of the room to make your notes.

Normal development

From observation, you will learn about normal child development, integrating theory with practice. You will study normal development so that you will understand what is unusual. It is obviously important to be able to assess children who may be behind in terms of physical, intellectual, social or emotional development, so that the childcare workers can help the child in the placement, or make a referral for specialist help. It is also important to be aware of the child who is advanced in some areas of development, so that a more stimulating programme can be planned.

Changes in behaviour

There might be a sudden change in the behaviour of a child. Careful observations are useful in this case, as the behaviour might have a physical cause, such as the onset of a bad cold, or it might be an emotional response to family problems.

It is necessary to understand that all children are individuals, and will behave and react differently in similar situations. Through close observation, you will be able to predict individual behaviour and reactions to situations, for example, understanding that one child might like to stroke a dog or cat while another would be too timid to do so, and you should respect both reactions.

Identifying good practice

Through observations you learn to identify good practice and become aware of your own role in seeing how other professionals meet the needs of children from many different backgrounds. The placement will benefit from your observations in the planning and reviewing of their practice.

You will not only observe individual children, but by looking at groups of children you will see different patterns of behaviour, and the interactions of the individuals within the groups.

Health care and safety

You will learn about health care and safety for all the children, and will become aware of their health needs and the dangers around them by observing carefully what happens in the placement, and being able to record it.

Children's needs

It is important to understand the needs of children, and to beome sensitive and perceptive in meeting these needs. It is only by recording objective observations that you can learn in a practical way how to become aware of these needs and how to meet them. It also shows you when the child is ready to move on to the next developmental stage. For example, a child walking holding on to furniture will be ready to use push-and-pull toys.

Students sometimes feel that colleges are setting up obstacles for them to overcome, but doing observations to a high standard is not a hurdle to be jumped but a contribution to a satisfying career. As a childcare worker, observing children will become second nature to you. You will have developed considerable skills in perception, both visual and aural, and will be able to record information clearly, concisely and accurately.

How to do observations

There are many different ways of doing observations, and in general the technique that you use will depend on the type of observation you wish to do. You can observe an individual child or a group of children. Whatever method you employ, you must try to be as objective as possible, and only record what you see.

You need to make yourself as inconspicuous as possible, sitting quietly with a pen and paper in a corner of the room. Your placement will give you time to do your observations in note form, and not expect you to take part in any activities while you are taking notes. Make sure all the staff in the room know what you are attempting, so there is less chance of you being interrupted. It is not good practice, generally speaking, to do observations involving yourself, so if the child or children insist on you taking part in what they are doing, give up, and try to observe later in the day. It is easier to start by observing just one child for a short period of time. Try to concentrate just on the child; it is seldom relevant to remark on the behaviour of adults. Detailed descriptions of activities which the children are involved in also have no place in your observation. Pretend you are wearing blinkers, and just look at the child!

When you have completed your notes, you should read them through to make sure they make sense, and then write them up in your own time. Your placement supervisor should set aside some time during the week to discuss your observations with you, and to sign them as a true record.

TITLE OF OBSERVATION _____

DATE: _____

Time observation started _____

Time observation completed _____

Name of child(ren) (first name only) _____

Age of child(ren) (years and months, e.g. 4:4) _____

Brief description of the setting (e.g. playground) _____

AIM OF OBSERVATION:
The aim of this observation is to observe a child/children:

_____

_____

DESCRIPTION (use present tense only):

COMMENT (What you have learnt from what you have observed –
          NOT HEARSAY)

_____

_____

Signed _____ (supervisor)

NEVER write a child's or a parent's full name, the name of nursery
staff or the name of the school on this form – this is unprofessional)

ALWAYS ask your supervisor to sign the observations and discuss
them with you before you bring them into college to show your
tutor.

Example format for an observation study

A written record

When you first start observing children, you will most likely use the method referred to as a written record. All the following things should be included:

- *Date*. This is important for two reasons. Firstly, you may be asked to present your observation file to the examiners in date order, so that they can see a progression in your work. Secondly, you may forget to make a note of the age of the child/children you are observing, but it will be easy to look up in the records if you have made a note of the date.

- *Name*. You should only use the first name of the child, or the initials. It would be a breach of confidentiality if you put the whole name. It is permissible to use a false name. For the same reason, you never name placement staff, but put 'the teacher' or 'the nursery nurse'. Obviously, the name of the placement never appears in your file.

- *Age*. Anyone reading your observation will want to know how old the child is so that they can see if the child is immature or advanced from the behaviour described in the observation.

- *Time observation started and finished*. Recording the length of time that you have observed is important for the reader.

- *Brief description of the setting*. (e.g. the outside play area). A child will behave quite differently outside riding the wheeled toys, than if he or she is sitting quietly in the book corner, and the reader will need to know the setting. If you observe a child who is moving rapidly from one area to another, you might at first decide to observe another child or do a very short observation, looking at the child using just one piece of equipment.

- *Aim of observation*. Before you start observing, it is a good idea to decide what it is you hope to observe. 'A 4 year-old using scissors, paper and glue', might be one idea, if you wanted to look at manipulative skills in a certain age group. Sometimes your college may ask you to do a particular observation to tie up with the theory your tutor may have been teaching. On the other hand, you might suddenly see an interesting event that you wish to observe. You would not have had an aim in the first place, and it is probably not necessary to invent one. It might look a little odd to put as your aim 'observing a child hurting herself on the climbing frame'!

- *Description*. Here you write your observation. You will always use the present tense, so that the reader can share in what is happening more easily.

- *Comment or evaluation.* This is the part which students find most difficult at first, but it is important to show what you have learnt from what you have observed. A good way to start is to look at the aim of the observation, and begin to link the comment with this. You must try not to make assumptions, using words like 'I think', or 'perhaps', and only comment on what you have actually seen. Reporting what your supervisors or other people might tell you about the child or the family background is not usually relevant to the observation, but if you are sure that it is, you put 'Following discussion with the supervisor/parent/ caregiver . . .' and then write what you have been told.

Guidelines on comments and evaluations

- Comment on the child/children's skills, use of toys and equipment, language and behaviour in relation to their age. Is it within the normal range, advanced or immature? (You should consult various books on child development and handouts from your college on the different ages; make comparisons with other children of the same age; discuss any difficulties with your training supervisor.)

- If the observation is of a child behaving in an unusual way, for example being very aggressive, or anxious, upset or clinging, note whether this is typical of that child, or very unusual. Your training supervisor may be able to suggest a possible reason for the behaviour.

- If the child has only recently started at the nursery, note the date of arrival in your comment. It takes some children quite a while to settle in to a new environment.

- The position of the child in the family may be relevant. Eldest children may be more used to adults, but more reluctant to leave the parent. Youngest children may be used to having their wishes anticipated for them by other members of the family, and find it difficult to be independent.

- If the language of the child at home is different from that of the placement, the child might find life very confusing at first, and become frustrated when unable to express his or her needs. This could lead to aggression or crying.

- It might be important to note the gender of the child if you feel it is relevant. Be careful not to express sexist attitudes; you should not be surprised if a girl enjoys rough play, or a boy wants to spend time in the home corner.

Examples of a written record

Example 1

TITLE: Physical development of the newborn baby
Date: 15th April 1991
Time started: 1.50 p.m.
Time completed: 2.05 p.m.
Name of child: Ben
Age of child: 9 weeks (Birthday 10.2.91)

The setting: the lounge in the home visited.

Aim of the observation: to observe physical development in the area of muscle control of the newborn.

Description:
Ben is sitting on his mother's lap, his head is in an upright position as he settles against her cradling arm.

Ben gazes around, momentarily focusing, then looks away to something else. He draws his fist to his face. The movement attracts his attention. He looks directly at his hand as the closed fist opens with extending fingers. His tongue protrudes, he makes slight cooing noises and his legs kick spontaneously. Furthermore, while still looking at his fingers, Ben attempts to draw his head forward. However, this movement unbalances his control; he wobbles and rests back against his mother.

Comment:
Ben is visually very alert and attentive to his surroundings, though seldom fixing continuously on an object. His head control still needs light support, but he can hold his head upright when cradled. His head tended to flop backwards when forward movements were attempted. Ben's limb movements are more deliberate and he is able to bring his hand to chin height. Such movements are evidence of his stage of development, indicating that he is best able to clearly focus within a visual field of 18–28 cm, and when opening his fists.

As he engages in the onset of finger play he demonstrates recognition of his body movements by a pleasurable response of slight vocalisations and rapid flexing of both legs. This form of play will be more apparent during his third month.

During this stage of Ben's development, his upper body control will be rapid, and self-play a newly-performed awareness.

Example 2

TITLE: Responses at Story-time
Date: 23.1.91
Time started: 11.30
Time completed: 11.44
Name of child: Daniel (Dan)
Age of child: 4 years, 4 months (9.9.86)

The setting: Book room

Aim of the observation: to observe a $4\frac{1}{2}$ year-old during a story using a prop.

Description:
'Forward folks', says T. 'That's it, now move back a wee bit'.
The children settle themselves in front of the flannel-graph (a story prop).
'Come on, Dan, come on Jason, move forward', says T.
There is further discussion as everyone gets ready. Dan has his thumb in his mouth, and his legs crossed.
T. holds up the book: *Rosie's Walk*.
'Who do you think Rosie is?' she asks.
'The chicken', everyone replies.
Dan takes his thumb out of his mouth, shuffles forward on his bottom, and puts his thumb back in. He shuffles some more, puts his finger in his mouth and leans forward.
'What way round should the rake be?' asks T.
'It has to be standing up', replies Dan.
Dan leans forward on his knees and shuffles into the middle of the group.
'I can see it', says Dan, in response to a general question.
The other children join in.
'I can see it', repeats Dan. He puts his thumb in his mouth.
'Dan, are you going to put the fox into the pond?' asks T.
'I can't see it', says Dan, getting to his feet.
He walks to the front, stepping over the children, chooses the pond from the pile of props, and sticks it on the board. He then picks up the fox, and puts it into the pond.
'His head can't stick on', says Dan.
'That's all right, go back and sit where you were sitting, Dan', says T.
The story continues.
'He jumps', says Dan.
Dan smiles as Jade puts the fox into the middle of the haystack.

'There's two little mouses', he says, pointing at the box.
'I haven't had a go', says Rachel.
'We can have another go after', says Dan to Rachel.
'Do you think Rosie knows the fox is following her?' asks T.
'I think she doesn't', says Dan. He puts his thumb back in his mouth and leans foward listening.
'I can see that, next to the white thing', says Dan, nodding his head in response to a general question to all.
'I saw them once on holiday', says Dan, talking about beehives.
Dan is up on his knees now.
'Is she under it?', Dan asks about Rosie.
'I think they're really fast' says Dan, regarding the bees. He fiddles with the waistband of his trousers.
Dan stands up as the last prop goes on the board and then sits down again.

Comment:
Dan clearly enjoys story-time. He follows the story well and remains interested and active throughout. He is inclined to interrupt the story but his comments are always relevant, and often he responds to a general question with the expected answer before the other children. His hearing and speech correspond to developmental norms, his tenses are correct, using past and present, and his grammar is good. He recalls past experiences, mentioning the beehives he saw, and although he fidgets a bit he is not disruptive. His concentration span is appropriate to his age and sucking his thumb is a comfort and helps him to relax and settle. He shows a sense of humour by smiling at the funny parts of the story.

As time goes on, you will find it easier to write your evaluations, and there is no reason why you should not look back at earlier ones and, dating your new entry, expand on what you first wrote. This type of observation will form the basis of your observation folder. However, there are other ways of recording information and you need to be sure of using these methods in an appropriate manner.

Written records are generally used by qualified members of staff to look at how well a child is settling in, and to make sure that all the children in the placement are developing well in all ways. These observations can then be shared with parents and caregivers, who might like to do some observations at home. Sometimes observations are kept in a file with the child's records, and may be passed on when the child attends school. Of course, the parent will have access to these records if he or she wishes. At times tutors and supervisors will write a comment on your observation, often posing a question such as 'Why do you think the child said . . .?' You should respond to this by enlarging on your original evaluation.

Child studies

These will vary according to the requirements of your tutors, but the one thing they will have in common is that they will all refer to one child, studied in depth over an extended period of time.

Some colleges might ask you to visit and observe a baby from birth until the age of 1, noting regularly the all-round development of the baby. This is particularly useful for students at colleges which do not always have placements with very young babies. These observations may be presented in your observation file, or may form the basis of a child study. The student should describe the child, look at the development and behaviour over a period of time, and then write a summary describing what they have learnt about this one particular child. It is always necessary to get the permission of the parent, and the advice of the supervisor, before starting any child study.

Child studies will give you a detailed objective knowledge of one child, and an insight into the uniqueness of the individual. You may share your study with the parent/caregiver, who may contribute to it.

Example front page for a Child Study

Observation of a young baby

First visit

Date _27. 10. 91_

First name _John_

Date of birth _23. 9. 91_

Sex _Male_

Place of birth _Local District Hospital_

Duration of pregnancy _39 weeks_

Pregnancy _The mother's own description was 'awful'. She had low blood pressure, morning sickness and fainted twice._

Labour _Natural birth - no painkillers. Apgar scale at birth 9/10._

Post-natal history _Baby slightly jaundiced, feeding well, showing normal signs. Phototherapy for 12 hours._

Birth weight _3.2 kg_

Birth length _55 cm_

Place in family _3/3 - first male_

Feeding method first 4 weeks _Breast_

Feeding method from 1 month _Breast_

Activity of baby when first visited _In mother's arms, looking around._

Activity of mother when first visited _Holding baby, cuddling and talking to him._

Any other information _Father present at birth, other children with family friend. Mother in hospital for two weeks before delivery & one week postnatally._

Developmental guide

Towards independence

Insert the date in the first two columns, and add your comments.

In supine, lies with head to one side, arm and leg on face side outstretched, or both arms flexed; knees apart, soles of feet turned inward.		
First accomplished:	**Performs well:**	**Comment:**
Pulled to sit, head lags until body vertical, when head is held momentarily erect before falling forwards.		
First accomplished:	**Performs well:**	**Comment:**
Held sitting, back is one complete curve.		
First accomplished:	**Performs well:**	**Comment:**

Checklists

Checklists or developmental guides are a quick way of presenting a great deal of information about a child of any age, from which to assess the child further and plan for extending the child's development. The list could encompass all areas of development, or could look at one specific area that the placement might be concerned about. The student will need to evaluate the checklist after completion, and decide if the child has any particular needs.

Checklists may be used for all the children in the placement on a regular basis, to enable the staff to plan for each child's needs. For example, a checklist may show that a child, although well within the average range for his or her age in physical development, nevertheless does not have one or two specific skills, such as using scissors. Once the staff are aware of this, opportunities to practise the skills and encouragement can be given to the child. A checklist could also show that a child is advanced in one area which had previously gone unnoticed, such as maturity in drawing ability, and this skill can be built on and extended.

Example of a Checklist

Developmental guide

Visit to a newborn baby

If possible, arrange to see the baby being fed, or bathed, rather than when asleep. Observe the baby carefully, noticing her/his behaviour. Watch the baby's eyes, her/his hands and feet; notice any sounds s/he makes.

Over a ten-minute period, check the following:	YES	NO
Does the baby look at the mother?		
Does s/he look away and then look back?		
Does s/he move his hands and arms?		
Does s/he kick with his feet?		
Does s/he move hands, arms and feet together?		
Does s/he cry during this period?		
Does s/he make any other noises?		
Ask the mother if s/he is breast fed?		
Is s/he still fed during the night?		
Does s/he cry during the night?		
Does this disturb the parents' rest?		

If there are any young children present, notice how they react to the baby. Note the ages of any other children.

Time samples

These are used to observe a child for a fixed period of time, for example, one minute every half-hour, for one or more days. The reason for doing this is concern about a child who appears to be withdrawn, unable to make relationships or unusually shy. By checking regularly to see who the child is with, and if he or she is relating in any way to another child or adult, it is possible to prove whether or not the child is really withdrawn and giving cause for anxiety, or just reserved and self-sufficient.

Time samples may also be used to see how children are using the toys and equipment in the placement. This is often helpful to the staff, who might think that all the equipment is being used equally, and then discover that some equipment is more popular than others. This could lead to enlarging or extending some areas of play.

Event samples

If you have a child in the placement who the staff feel is very aggressive or disruptive, you might need to find out if this is really so, and if any of the behaviour is provoked by other children or even by members of staff. It is very easy to presume that one child is the root cause of all disturbances, and staff have been known to shout out a child's name if there is a fight and then discover the child is absent that day. By noting all events that occur over one or several days, it is possible to have a truer picture of the child, and what might be causing his or her distress.

Time and event samples are used in placement to detect if children have a real behaviour problem or if it is just the perception of the staff. If the samples show that the child needs help, these sort of observations are often presented to the people offering professional help. Sometimes these observations are used in case conferences, where the future of the child is being discussed by a team of professional people. If the problem is not as serious as was first thought, the sample might show the staff that the way the child is being managed may be contributing in some way to the child's distress. The sample will enable the whole team to sit down together and see how the child can be helped in the placement to resolve a temporary anxiety.

Time sample

(This type of observation should be used for a child who is withdrawn or having difficulty in making and/or sustaining relationships.)

Name: Simon

First language: English

Age: 2:4

Position in family: Eldest

Gender: M

Length of time in nursery: 10 months

The problem: Simon rarely talks. Sits alone & thumbsucks Twiddles his hair. Appears not to make relationships

Time	Setting	Language	Social group
8:30	Cloakroom. Simon arrives with mother.	Clings to mother. Sucks thumb.	Simon, Mother N. Worker
9.0	Playroom. Sitting on carpet, rocking.	None	/
9:30	Playroom. Having a cuddle, listening to story.	Looking at book "What's that?"	Simon + N.W.
10.0	Playroom. Sitting on chair drinking juice.	None	Small group
10.30	Garden. Standing alone sucking thumb.	None	Alone in large group
11.0	Playroom. Home corner. Role playing a baby.	Listening to Sandra 3:6	Simon & Sandra
11.30	Bathroom area. Sitting on lavatory.	Humming to himself. Twiddling hair	Alone
12.0	Dining area. Sitting at table, eating.	"More cake?"	Participating in large group

Event sample/frequency count

Date: 10·10·91
Name: Anne
Age: 3:8
Gender: F

First language: English
Position in family: 2nd child
Length of time in nursery: Two terms

The problem: Anne is disruptive and aggressive towards adults and her peer group.

Day of week	Number of event	Duration	Provoked/ Unprovoked	Comments on seriousness of behaviour
Monday	1	2-3 mins	U.P.	Disrupted group during milk & biscuit time by lying on the floor & singing loudly.
Monday	2	2 mins	U.P.	'Rugby' tackle' on adult's leg.
Monday	3	2 mins	U.P.	Hit another child on the face with a wooden brick.
Monday	4	2-3 times at 10-15 minute intervals	U.P.	Stands in front of T.V. until other children react.
Tuesday	1	2-3 mins	U.P.	Hit adult on the back quite hard while adult was listening to another child. Adult asked Anne to stop as it hurt, when other child had finished adult would listen to Anne.
Tuesday	2	2 mins	U.P.	Tried to poke another child in the eyes with her fingers.

Taped language samples

When you are studying language development in college, your tutor may ask you to tape a child who is either fluent or delayed in speech. These tapes can then be put in your observation folder, with comments and evaluation.

There are difficulties in employing this technique. First of all, you need the permission of the placement and the parent. Secondly, you must be competent in handling the tape recorder without being too obvious in your use of it, as this will inhibit the child. Before attempting the actual recording, you will need to practise at home. Thirdly, there will be a degree of background noise in most placements, but you will probably be better taping the child in the familiar environment rather than taking him or her out to a quieter place. Short language samples are better recorded carefully using the written report technique. Remember to use inverted commas when writing such reports.

The tapes may be used with children who are thought to have language delay or immature speech. If the child is later referred to a speech therapist, the dated tapes will be most useful in showing any progress. Speech therapists will often ask childcare workers either to tape a child's language or to record a sample in writing, as children are likely to be more relaxed and confident with a known member of staff than with a stranger.

Movement charts and sociograms

This is another shorthand way of presenting information about an individual or a group of children. A movement chart might be used to see how a child uses the placement equipment, by drawing a plan of the room, and indicating with arrows the child's movement around the room. A sociogram is often used to indicate the relationships within a group of children. The following example shows how a sociogram can be compiled.

TITLE OF OBSERVATION: SOCIAL DYNAMICS

Date:7/5/91
Time observation started: 09.30
Time observation completed: 12.30
Names of children:As on graph
Ages of children: 5:9 to 7:8
Description of setting: Middle and top infant classroom.

The aim of this observation is to observe the childrens' relationships with each other.

I asked the children to draw me a picture of their three best friends, and compiled the following graph to show the results. I only included those children in the class on the graph.

Comment

The graph shows that in general the children chose same-sex friends, with a few exceptions. The girls were more inclined to name a boy as a friend than the boys were a girl.

George (7:7), Victor (7:4) and Maz (7:7), who polled most votes, are amongst the oldest children in the class. Of these three, Maz's votes came entirely from boys. He is often in trouble at school because of his behaviour, and can be quite aggressive, traits that make some of the boys look up to him, and the girls avoid him.

Of the children who polled no votes, Rafik, Sara and Winston have only been in the class five weeks, having come up from Reception. Sara is a rather timid, often tearful girl who tends to stick close to Louise, who came from Reception with her, and was absent today. Winston chose his twin brother, Roger, and older sister, Emma as his best friends. He is rather quiet, and tends to seek them out in the playground rather than join in with his classmates. Rafik nominated the three boys who were sitting at his table at the time. None of these three have established themselves in the class, and would not be expected to have formed firm relationships within the group yet. Of the other two children who failed to get a vote, Danny (7:3) is again a quiet child who is frequently absent (as he was today), making it difficult to form relationships, and Sharon (7:8), who has quite marked behavioural problems, is often argumentative and aggressive. This would seem to show that such behaviour is seen as more acceptable in boys than in girls, even at this young age.

The children who chose each other tended to be amongst the older group, which is as expected as special friends tend to be made at 7 years, although I was surprised that this was more common amongst the boys. They tend to play and work together in a group, as is commonly seen at this age, but I would have expected to see more evidence of special friendships amongst the girls. Tara (7.5) proved most popular amongst the girls, but was absent today.

Most of the children seem to interact reasonably well together, although the few disruptive children can have an adverse effect on the whole group.

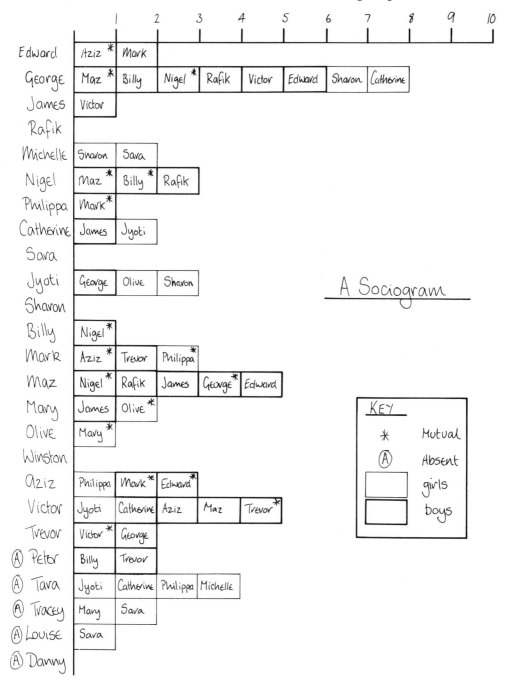

A Sociogram

Graphs, pie and bar charts

These can be a useful way of collating information which you might need to have about a group of children. For example, what shoes do children wear on arrival at school? What is the most used piece of inside or outside equipment? Does the age of a child relate to his or her skill with a knife and fork?

Sometimes these graphs and charts can be used in reports to managers, giving information about the placement in an easy-to-digest format. Parents can use pie charts at home, colouring in a child's ability to acquire certain skills, and sharing the information with the placement. Charts showing the use the children are making of the equipment provided might help staff to encourage children to use other types of equipment, perhaps putting out more stimulating material.

It may be hard to believe now, but many students will enjoy using all the different methods of observation, and feel proud of their professional skill.

All observations should be objective records of children's development and behaviour and can therefore be valued and trusted. You, as a professional with a specific skill, will be equally valued and trusted. You will find that observation is a case of practice makes perfect!

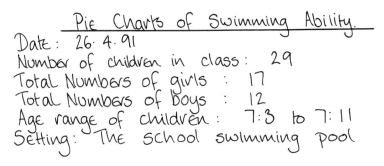

Pie Charts of Swimming Ability.

Date: 26. 4. 91
Number of children in class: 29
Total Numbers of girls : 17
Total Numbers of boys : 12
Age range of children : 7:3 to 7:11
Setting: The school swimming pool

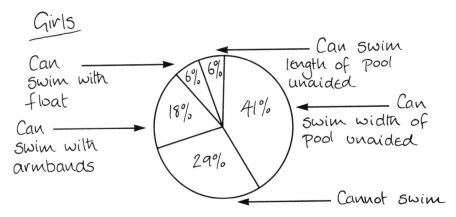

Girls

Can swim with float

Can swim with armbands

6% 6%

18% 41%

29%

Can swim length of pool unaided

Can swim width of pool unaided

Cannot swim

Boys

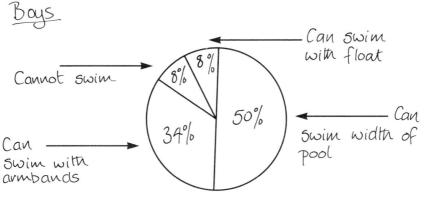

Can swim
with float

Cannot swim

8%
8%

Can
swim width of
pool

50%

34%

Can
swim with
armbands

ACTIVITY

How would you comment on the above information?

ACTIVITY

What comment would you make about the use of table activities in the nursery featured in this bar graph?

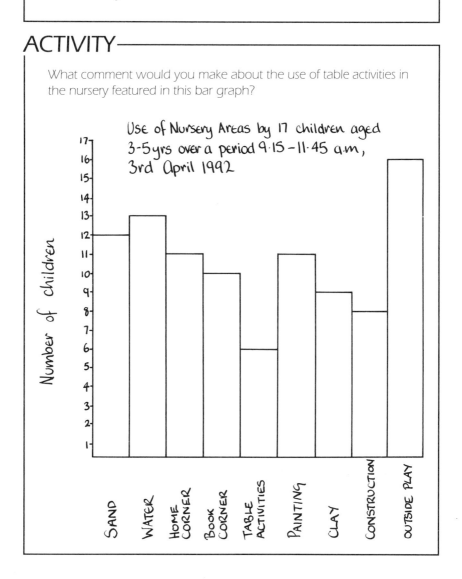

Use of Nursery Areas by 17 children aged
3-5 yrs over a period 9.15 – 11.45 a.m,
3rd April 1992

Number of children

7 Health and Safety

Under the 1974 Health and Safety at Work Act employers have a duty to provide healthy and safe working conditions. This chapter does not attempt to describe the total responsibilities of any placement in providing such an environment. It is intended as a guide for the student who will be supervised at all times, but nevertheless be expected to make a contribution towards establishing a healthy and safe environment for the children and staff.

When you start working in any placement you will need to find out the answers to the questions in the following checklists as soon as possible:

Check list   **Fire**

What is the procedure to follow should a fire occuur?

Where are the fire alarms?

What type of alarm is used?

How are the children taken from the building?

What exits are used? Under what circumstances?

Where do you gather outside the building?

Where are the registers kept? (The children's names need to be checked when everyone is out of the building.)

There should be regular fire drills to make sure everyone knows what to do in the event of a fire.

Check list   **Accidents**

What is the procedure to follow should an accident occur?

Where is the first aid box kept?

Who has a first aid qualification, or who is the appointed person to take charge in the event of an accident?

Where is the nearest telephone?

Every accident, however slight, should be reported and recorded in the accident book. Ask your supervisor if you can look at the book. You will see that very full details are recorded. This information is necessary as some seemingly minor accidents can result in more serious concerns, and accurate recording can be vital. The accident book may also show hazards that occur regularly. Remember too that parents must be informed of any injury, however slight it may seem.

Check list

Other essential information

What is the procedure concerning storage and administration of medicine? (Not all placements are prepared to accept this responsibility.)

Do any of the doors exit on to a main road? Is there a procedure for making sure children do not have access to this?

What is the procedure for dealing with the outbreak of infection?

How is the outside play area set up? Find out how risks from falls and collisions are minimised in and out of doors.

Check list

Student welfare

Where are the staff toilets?

Where is the staffroom?

Is there a room which can be used if a member of staff is unwell?

Where can you eat in the building?

Are you able to buy food in the placement?

What are your hours of duty?

Does your supervisor know who to contact should you be unwell or have an accident?

Check list

Hazards

Are any of the toys or items of equipment damaged or faulty?

Is there any unstable furniture?

Are there any electrical points uncovered, trailing wires, faulty wiring?

Are cleaning substances and medicines kept locked away, out of the reach of the children?

Are there any hidden areas outside, where children cannot be seen?

Are electric kettles and mugs or cups of hot fluid kept out of the children's reach?

Are there any plants or pets which are harmful to children?

Are there any obstructions in corridors and doorways?

Are fire doors ever propped open?

Is rubbish and paper left lying around, increasing the fire risk?

Is outdoor play equipment regularly checked for safety?

All children are entitled to a clean, safe, pleasant, caring environment. As a student, you can contribute to this by being alert to hazards, and giving thought to your practice. If you have identified a problem or hazard discuss it with your supervisor as soon as possible.

ACTIVITY

1 Identify indoor and outdoor plants that might be poisonous.

2 Investigate diseases which are associated with pets.

Good practice

1 Ensure that the rooms are aired regularly, and that a temperature of 20 °C is maintained.

2 The eating area should be clean, attractive and free from any debris. Clean up well after meals.

3 Change any child who is wet at once, maintaining personal hygiene. Ensure that soiled clothing and napkins are disposed of hygienically.

4 Do not allow small areas of the room to become overcrowded or cluttered. Organise activities so that noise levels are controlled.

5 Maintain clean, soft area where children can rest on pillows or rugs.

6 Shut gates and doors properly behind you.

7 Use stair gates where appropriate.

8 Wipe spills of water or food at once, and do not allow the children to walk on floors recently washed in case they slip.

9 Keep pets in a healthy condition, regularly cleaning cages and hutches.

10 Prevent children in outside play areas from talking to strangers who may attempt to attract their attention.

11 Regularly wash dressing-up clothes and cushion covers, toys and equipment.

12 Make sure that children work and play in well-lit areas.

Personal health and hygiene

There are many definitions of health. The World Health Organisation states that 'Health is a state of complete physical, mental and social well-being, not merely the absence of disease or infirmity'. It involves children, families, and the community, and is a positive goal, not just the absence of illness.

You should present yourself as a good role model, and encourage the children to think about their health in a positive way. Much of your theory at college will look at the concept of health and health education. This knowledge should be demonstrated and displayed in your practice at all times.

Good practice

1 Encourage all children to wash their hands after using the lavatory, before eating and before taking part in cooking activities.

2 Play your part in making sure the lavatories are always clean and that soap and paper towels are available.

3 Dispose of rubbish such as dirty napkins or tissues promptly and correctly.

4 Wear sensible shoes with flat heels for work, and encourage parents to send children to placement with practical shoes and appropriate clothing. Tracksuits both make it easier for children to use the toilets and allow for freedom of movement on the outside equipment.

5 Be careful not to lift anything that is too heavy for you. This also applies to children lifting things.

6 Do not allow smoking in the same room as the children.

7 If you are responsible for food preparation, remember the importance of clean working surfaces and utensils, strict personal hygiene and hygienic food storage. Do not handle food if you have an infected cut or diarrhoea.

8 Encourage children to cover their mouths if they cough.

9 Teach children to blow their noses with a tissue, and dispose of it correctly.

10 You may well come into contact with children who have rubella (German measles). If you are a young woman, planning to have a family later in life, check that you are immune to rubella before starting the course. If you have not been immunised and contract rubella during pregnancy there is a risk of your baby being damaged.

11 Encourage parents to think about immunisation for their children.

12 Some activities in the placement are potentially dangerous. Children working with wood or cooking should be closely supervised at all times. Fire is an obvious hazard. Make sure gas taps are switched off and do not leave tea towels or matches lying around. Use gloves to lift pans and turn handles away from the front of stoves. Discuss these activities thoroughly with your supervisor beforehand so that you are alerted to all the risks.

13 Keep up with new research and developments, for example the risk of covering fatty food with cling film.

Stress in the placement

Stress may be experienced by you in the following four areas:

● You feel that you're being asked to take on responsibilities and tasks before being fully prepared for them.

- There may be a conflict in the relationship between you and the supervisor.
- You may not understand exactly what is required, and be unclear about the expectations of the college and the supervisor.
- You do not enjoy the work.

Common symptoms of stress are headaches, insomnia, indigestion, irritability and possibly depression. If you feel stressed, you must discuss it with your personal tutor, who should be prepared to look at the problem with you. Often a visit to the placement by the tutor and a discussion with you and the supervisor together can resolve the difficulty. Very occasionally students do come to realise that they have made the wrong career choice, and decide to change courses.

A healthy and safe environment is essential to the well-being of children and adults. As you develop your skills and knowledge, you will understand that good childcare practice includes the prevention of accidents and illness, and being prepared to deal with emergencies in a calm, organised and confident manner.

8 Working with 0–3 Year-olds

During your training you will spend some time working with babies and toddlers from birth to three years. This could be in a family setting, in local authority day-care centres, community nurseries, workplace nurseries and crèches, or (for a few students) in the obstetric ward of hospitals. We will be looking at working with families in the next chapter.

Local authority day-care centres

The provision of places in day-care centres will vary from area to area, the more urban areas of the United Kingdom generally providing more places than the rural areas. Even so, there are long waiting lists for places, and this country has a poor record for providing inexpensive group care provision for babies and young children. There are very few places offered for young babies, mainly because it is felt that most young babies are better cared for in a family setting, either at home or, if this is not possible, with a childminder. Because there is such a shortage of places, these are allocated to families who have the greatest need. Referrals will come from social workers, health visitors, general practitioners and other professionals who feel the child will benefit from such provision. Some places are kept for the children of single parents, so that the parent can be free to work. With the ever-increasing demand, arising from parents wishing to work, there is a considerable shortage of places for these families. Some places will be used by social services as part of a programme for child protection.

The team

Many centres will employ a multi-disciplinary team, with social workers, nursery nurses, nursery teachers, playskills workers, registered general nurses, and experienced workers with no formal qualifications. With the introduction of National Vocational Qualifications many of these workers will have the opportunity of demonstrating their competence and gaining a recognised qualification.

The centre's day

Many centres are open from early morning until about 6 p.m., five days a week and 50 weeks a year. The staff will work shifts to cover the day and the year. This necessitates a large number of staff, and can be confusing for the children (as well as the student!). Some centres operate a 'key worker' system, where one member of staff will be responsible for three or four children, and will be involved with the families of these children. In some centres there will be an emphasis on working with the family, particularly those where the child is at risk, and encouraging parents to take part in the day-to-day life of the centre and the care of the children, gaining confidence in their parenting skills. The student in this situation will need a mature, professional approach and understanding of the stresses that some families face.

Books and toys available

Carpet area

The sofa, flowers, fish and carpet create a homely atmosphere

A well-organised room for toddlers

Community nurseries

These are usually set up by local community groups with a special interest or need. For example, parents living on a large estate and feeling isolated with their young children may press for a nursery for the children, and for their own social needs. Alternatively, it might be a group of parents from the same cultural background, who wish their children to be cared for together, maintaining a sense of their cultural identity.

Finance

In general, groups approach the local authority for a grant, for premises, and for help and advice, but they remain independent, establish their own aims and objectives, and are run by a management committee of parents and local interested people. Most would employ qualified and unqualified staff, sometimes parents helping on a voluntary basis. Because the local authority demands more staff when babies are admitted (usually one member of staff for every three babies) it is not easy for parents to get a place, even in their own community, for very young babies, unless there is an urgent need.

Workplace nurseries and crèches

Workplace nurseries might be run by large institutions such as hospitals and universities for their staff and students, shared by businesses such as banks, manufacturing and television companies for their staff, or set up by a franchise company which will make sure that the same standard of care is used throughout their schemes.

The nurseries are provided to ensure that companies keep valued and well-trained staff, and expect to have many more young babies as the mothers return to work after maternity leave. The nurseries may be run by a management team of parents, staff and representatives of the employer. With more women entering the workforce every year, and delaying starting a family until established in their career, there is an ever-increasing demand for places.

Obstetric units in hospitals

Some colleges are able to place students in this type of placement to work with mothers and new born babies. It is unfortunate that there are decreasing numbers of opportunities for students to have this experience, owing to the other training commitments of hospitals.

Students will spend the majority of their time on the wards, helping mothers to care for their babies. It is a very valuable experience. The student has to bear in mind that he or she is there to help the mother–baby bonding, and to aid in the development of the mother's parenting skills, such as bathing, day-to-day care and feeding.

Some time might be spent in a special care baby unit, with more vulnerable babies. This would be an interesting experience, and students should work closely with the midwives in providing intensive care. They will also play a part in helping parents come to terms with the situation, and to relate to their babies.

Good practice   ## In day-care centres

1   Listening and responding to very young children is a priority. Some time should be spent with them every day on a one-to-one basis, as well as in a group.

2   Books should be available at all times, and care should be taken to choose those most suitable for the age-group. A book looked at with a caring adult not only stimulates language, but also helps build a loving relationship.

3   All children need stimulating play, however young.

4   Children in napkins should be changed as soon as the napkins become wet or soiled. They are particularly vulnerable to infection, especially in a group situation, and care should be taken to prevent the spread of infection.

5   Children should be allowed to sleep at the time they wish to, and not have to fit in with the daily routine.

6   Toilet training should only take place after discussion with the parents and when the child shows he or she is ready to be trained, and not to fit in with the daily routine.

7   The 'key worker' system, where one member of staff relates more closely to a child and the family, helps build a relationship of care and trust and ensures continuity between home and the nursery.

8   A good understanding of the dietary needs of the individual child is required. Liaise closely with parents and bear in mind the developmental stage of the child, and the cultural and ethnic background of the family.

9   All children need activities which will extend and stimulate their development and therefore a sound knowledge of developmental 'norms' is necessary. Any developmental delay can be picked up early, and an appropriate referral made. Clear records and observations need to be kept and shared with the family.

ACTIVITY

1   Try some messy play with paint, sand or water. The younger the child, the more the mess, as they like to use their whole bodies in the activity.

2   Rhymes and finger play appropriate to the age-group should be used on a regular basis, either in a very small group, or individually. Ask your supervisor and your friends to help you collect as many rhymes as you can.

3   Young children enjoy listening and dancing to music. Find some suitable tapes. If you play an instrument, take it into the placement and use it with the children.

4   Books should be read whenever a child wants. Compile a suitable list of books for very young children with the help of your tutor or your local library.

The person who wishes to work with very young children should be particularly warm, caring and responsive, and aware of the vulnerability of such young children in all areas of development.

9 Working in the Family Placement

Many students, when qualified, will want to work as nannies. Ideally the family placement should have two or three children, with one child under one year of age. This not only provides more experience for you, but ensures that the parent or carer is experienced and confident in taking on the supervision of the student.

Preparation

There has to be a certain amount of discussion between the family, the college and the student before starting a family placement. There may be a preliminary meeting at the college, so that you can meet the carer and the children before starting the placement. Many questions can be asked and answered at this meeting, for example who would pay the fares on a visit, and is insurance cover provided for the student? Mealtimes may be a problem, as some families will provide food, while others expect the student to bring a packed lunch. It could be a question of finance, or of special diets. The timing of the day can be flexible in order to meet the family's needs and to allow you maximum time with the children.

Fitting in

Working with families is quite different from working in an establishment such as a day-care centre or a school. All families vary in lifestyle, child-rearing practices, expectations of the skills of the student, attitude to smoking, ways in which they control their children, diet, routine, bedtimes, religion, cultural background, amount of involvement in play, going on outings, television-watching, noise levels, pets, housing ... the list is endless. Obviously you have to be flexible, and feel confident enough to enjoy the experience of a different way of life. A professional attitude is essential in a family placement. You will need to be punctual, as the children can be very disappointed if you do not arrive when expected, and the parent or carer might feel very let-down if an outing has been planned with you in mind.

Confidentiality

When you are in close daily contact with a family you will become aware
of confidential information and private family matters, and it is
important that these are not discussed with other students, tutors or
friends. The only exception to this would be if you felt that one of the
children was at risk in any way, and this must obviously be discussed at
once with your tutor. This would be a very rare occurrence but in this
situation the tutor has a responsibility to you and to the child.

What the family placement can offer you

This placement can offer you the opportunity to:

- work with and observe children of varying ages in the home
- see children in a variety of situations
- discuss the health and development of the children with a very
  involved and interested adult
- attend the sort of outings that children go on with their parents
  or carers, such as to the infant welfare clinic, to the swimming
  baths, visiting other families

- see how the older children react at home after spending time in school or nursery
- see how other families function, and the stress and the pleasure that young children bring.

What you can offer to the placement

You can:

- assist with all aspects of the children's physical care, such as bathing, feeding, exercise, and possibly caring for them during ill-health
- create a stimulating environment for the children, initiating new play ideas, and giving advice on suitable toys and equipment
- help with the essential chores, such as doing the children's laundry, preparing and clearing away children's meals, maintenance of clothes and equipment, and cleaning the children's bedrooms
- bring to the family the current theories about childcare and development issues
- provide companionship for the parent or carer and the children, with a friendly caring attitude
- do observations of the children, to share with the family.

ACTIVITY

1 Visit the infant welfare clinic with the family. What routine checks are carried out? What advice is given to the parent or carer?

2 Research in local shops the next major piece of equipment to be bought, looking at quality, price and safety.

3 Plan a suitable family outing, taking into account transport, cost and the value to the children.

Possible problems

If you and the family have had plenty of opportunity to gain prior knowledge of each other, problems are unlikely to occur. There have been occasions, however, when the family expectations have not matched those of the college. This may be because:

- the family treats you as an extra pair of hands, and you are expected to take on domestic chores for the whole family

- you are not given the opportunity to observe and discuss the progress of the children
- you lack tact, and criticise child-rearing practices
- you feel uneasy in the house. This might be, for example, because of the lack of hygiene, or the unwelcome attentions of a member of the household
- the day seems endless, as the baby sleeps most of the time, the older children are at school, and there is just not enough to do
- there is a great deal of stress in the household, and you feel unable to cope, and that too much is expected of you
- attitudes expressed in the household are in conflict with your set of values
- a parent or carer objects to the standard of care you provide.

Tutors should be in frequent contact with you during this time and anxieties should be expressed as soon as possible. Tutors will visit and attempt to resolve difficulties, but if this is not possible, a new placement will have to be found.

However, most students really enjoy this type of placement, and for some it will confirm their future career choice. A happy loving family, even if different from one's own, provides a fulfilling and satisfying placement. Many students will form lasting friendships with the parents or carers and the children, and continue to visit them for many years.

10 Working with 3–5 Year-olds

During your training and career, you will be working with 3–5 year-olds in a number of different settings. Each establishment may have different aims for the children, and therefore your role as a carer will vary to some degree.

Nursery education

Nursery schools

These usually cater for children from $2\frac{1}{2}$ to 5 years old, are staffed by a head teacher, nursery teachers, and nursery nurses. The children may stay for the morning, the afternoon, or all day, usually between 9 a.m. and 3 p.m. The ideal is to have one member of staff for every eight children, but staff/child ratios will vary according to the local education authority. During their time at nursery school the children will be encouraged to become independent people, developing physically, socially, emotionally and intellectually, with perhaps more emphasis on intellectual and language development in some schools.

Nursery class

These usually occupy the same hours and have the same aims as a nursery school. There may be fewer staff, usually just one nursery teacher and one nursery nurse for every 25 children. The head teacher will be in charge of the primary school as well as the nursery class. The nursery team will be part of the larger primary school team and the aims and philosophies of the school may have an effect on the nursery class.

The team
The nursery teacher is generally in charge, and the nursery nurse, while playing a most valuable part as a member of the team, works directly to the nursery teacher. The nursery nurse will be expected to be responsible for the care and health of the children and for implementing the curriculum. In a good team, all the staff will work together to achieve the best for all the children, and different members of the team will have different responsibilities.

Day-care

Day-care placements vary, but will usually have facilities for children from 8 a.m. to 6 p.m. The 3–5 year-olds may have a playroom of their own which they may use for some part of the day away from the younger children. The childcare worker has a much greater say in the educational input, and more responsibility in every way. As the day is longer, the pace of the day needs to be slower. The ratio of staff to children will be about one to five, but there has to be some allowance made for shift work, staff breaks and annual leave. The aims of the placement may put more emphasis on the all-round care of the child, and in some cases of the whole family.

The team

In a day-care centre, some of the staff will be qualified nursery nurses and others may be experienced staff with little formal training. There may also be staff who have social work qualifications, counselling diplomas, or some other background, making up a multi-disciplinary team. As the day is longer, the staff will work shifts, covering the day from 7.30 a.m. to 6.00 p.m. for 50 weeks of the year, but this may vary from area to area. Holiday time is less, the hours may be longer, but the salary is higher, the opportunities for promotion are much better, and the responsibilities often greater.

Playgroups

Playgroups also vary, some offering full-time daycare, but the vast majority are run on a sessional basis, and the parent will choose how often the child will attend; it could be every morning, one or two mornings a week, or both morning and afternoon sessions every day. A few playgroups have nursery nurses in charge, many have staff with a Pre-school Playgroup Association (PPA) certificate, others are run entirely by unqualified staff. The parents are generally involved in the running of the group, both in the day-to-day activities, and in the management. Most playgroups were started because there was not enough provision for young children in the area. The aims are mainly social, giving local children a chance to play together. The hours may be shorter, the pay will certainly be lower and the responsibility will be shared with the parents.

Location

A playgroup often operates in a building shared by other groups in the community. This means that at the end of each session each user of the hall has to clear away all their equipment, and this can be quite trying for the playgroup staff, and may limit some of the messier activities that should be offered to under-fives, such as using clay or finger-painting.

Play

In an ideal group, there should be many activities offered so that the needs of all the children in the group are met, and all areas of their development are extended. Before you take on the responsibility for planning any activities, you should check with your supervisor to make sure that, firstly, they fit in with the plan for the week, and secondly, that they are suitable for the age-group and safe for the children.

Activities outside

Outside there should be places to climb and wheeled toys to ride, and a large area to run and jump around in. Fresh air and exercise should be available all day so that the children have a choice of stimulating play outside or inside the room. Digging and planting will help children's arm muscles to develop as well as giving them a direct interest in their environment. Private places in the garden where children can feel safe and secure and away from adult eyes (they think!) give children time for reflection and for sharing with one special friend, so aiding their social and emotional development. Many imaginative games take place outside, as well as ring games and ball games. Positional vocabulary is developed, as children learn the words for climbing under and over equipment, up and down, in and out.

Equipment to balance on

Equipment to go over

Equipment to go under

Equipment to go through

An example of an 'assault course' for young children

ACTIVITY

1 Draw a plan of your placement room and the outside area, showing where all the activities take place.

2 Set up an 'assault course' that is challenging yet safe for the children. This must be carefully supervised.

3 Make the children a den using triangle apparatus covered with blankets or sheets. Observe the difference in some children's play when they feel they are not being watched.

Activities inside

Inside, there should be areas of quiet and areas of more noisy activity. The book area should be comfortable and safe, with a wide variety of books covering familiar and new stories and traditional tales, together with factual books giving information and books for helping children with emotional problems. These books should not only reflect the cultural mix of the children in the group, but other cultures as well. All books must be scrutinised, whether received as a gift, borrowed from the library, or bought from funds, to make sure that the illustrations as well as the text are neither sexist, classist or racist.

ACTIVITY—————————————————

1 Read suitable short stories to a small group of children as often as possible.

2 Set up a hospital ward. It is important to use realistic equipment, such as bandages, stethoscopes and kidney dishes. Syringes without needles are useful for pretend injections. This sort of play is most therapeutic for children who may have had a distressing hospital experience, or for those who may be going into hospital.

The home corner

The home corner should also reflect different cultures from around the world, both in dressing-up clothes and in domestic equipment. Saris, Chinese children's jackets, African cloth, woks and chopsticks are just a few examples. Here the play will be domestic, reflecting the family at home in the case of the younger children, and will develop into truly imaginative play as the children reach five. Children benefit from playing different roles in both domestic and imaginative play.

Using natural materials

Natural materials such as water, dry sand, wet sand, clay and mud should be available for the children every day. Sometimes play dough can be added. These materials do not break, return to their own form after use, and do not demand any end-product from the children. At an early age, they should be handled without tools or equipment, allowing the children to explore their properties for themselves. This is the beginning of early scientific learning, as well as being a safe area from which to watch the rest of the busy classroom.

ACTIVITY

1 Add vegetable dye to water to make it look more interesting, or washing-up liquid to produce soap bubbles. These should not be used if there are children allergic to soap or detergent in the group. This play can be extended by adding plastic tubing for blowing and whisks for beating.

2 Add sand wheels, balances and sieves to dry sand. Spades, moulds and blocks encourage creative play with wet sand. Imaginative play is stimulated by adding small world toys such as farm animals, cars and people.

3 Look at different recipes for play dough and make some with the children.

Creative activities

Creative activities stimulate children to experiment with different materials as well as encouraging language development, decision making, problem-solving, and co-operating and sharing with others. Learning to wait for the scissors or the sticky tape helps children to realise that other people have to be considered. Manipulative skills develop, as children learn to cut and to print. Junk modelling, collage, and the many ways of using paint all help the children to discover for themselves how to use these materials. No end-product should ever be demanded from the younger children, as this may curtail their creativity and the delight they get from experimenting with many sorts of materials. If a result is always demanded, the child may feel discouraged from exploring all that is on offer. The adult should be careful not to make models for the children to copy as this will lessen the children's confidence, and they will feel that their own efforts are not worthwhile.

ACTIVITY

1 Cornflour mixed to a certain consistency with a little water will feel dry to the touch, but when poured out on to a hard surface will turn runny. Children enjoy experimenting with this 'magic'.

2 All types of junk can be used for model making, as well as in collage. Collect all sizes and shapes of boxes, from large cartons to matchboxes. Tubes and cylinders (not the insides of lavatory rolls, as this is unhygienic), spheres and circles, scraps of material and paper: all these things and many more will help the children to make imaginative models.

Paints

Paints should always be available for the children to use whenever they feel like expressing their thoughts and feelings in a painting. Children with limited fluency in language often find it therapeutic to express themselves in paint. Adults should never ask a child about spontaneous paintings, as they are usually an expression of feelings that the child cannot yet put into words, but you should always have time to listen if a child wishes to talk about a painting. Some children rarely paint, while others feel it is the only way to start the day, and may do several paintings one after the other.

Painting allows children to look at the variety of different colours by mixing paints themselves. Children should be allowed to choose from a selection of paper of varying types and shapes.

Musical instruments

Musical instruments should always be there for the use of the children. Include instruments made in the nursery. Instruments, records, dances, and songs from countries all round the world will add interest and enjoyment, as well as showing appreciation and respect for different cultures. Musical experiences aid the imagination, soothe aggressive feelings and allow children to express themselves, which is especially helpful to those children whose language may be delayed or limited. Moving to music and using instruments leads to good muscle development. Singing in a group is a social activity, shared by children and staff. Dancing together helps children to co-operate with one another, as well as being tremendous fun.

ACTIVITY

You can help the children to make their own musical instruments, and this will help them to understand how sounds are made. All types of containers can be used to make simple shakers, and different fillings will give very different sounds, salt sounding soft and soothing, large beans or pebbles giving a much louder strident tone.

Jigsaws and other toys
Children will enjoy playing with a variety of jigsaws, table-top toys, bricks and large and small construction apparatus. This will be the start of early reading and mathematics, and will help develop children's hand–eye co-ordination.

Cooking

Cooking in the classroom is educational as well as fun. If the children participate all the way through the activity, from shopping for the ingredients to eating the end result, a great deal will have been learnt. Both mathematics and science will be involved in the weighing of ingredients, choosing the cooking equipment, measuring and counting, and the transformation of the uncooked ingredients into the finished dish. Many concepts will have been absorbed through the children's own experimentation and experience. Dishes from all round the world can be tried out, and sometimes parents may want to be involved in passing on their own expertise.

Outings

In many nursery groups, there will be opportunities for short outings, either in the immediate locality, or involving a short ride on public transport. You will be encouraged to take part in these outings. A visit to the local supermarket with one or two children provides an excellent learning opportunity for small children. This is best carried out when there is no rush or hurry to get home.

Pets

There may also be the opportunity to keep pets in the nursery, and some children will not be allowed pets at home. Handling pets and learning to be responsible for their care is a step towards independence, learnt in the security of the nursery. You need to make sure that no child or member of staff is allergic to any type of pet.

ACTIVITY

On the plan of the room and the outside area which you have already drawn, showing where all the activities take place, have you included everything mentioned in this chapter? Is there anything in your nursery that has not been mentioned? If you were responsible for the setting up of the area, is there anything you might rearrange? If so, why?

Check list

Have you:

prepared any creative activities?

read or told a story to a group of children?

led a music session?

cooked with the children?

initiated any outside play activities?

added anything to the home corner?

taken part in any imaginative play?

set up any activities with natural materials?

been on any outings or visits with the children and staff?

become involved in team discussions, contributing your own suggestions?

taken part in the assessment of any children?

kept up-to-date with your observations?

Three and four year-olds are a delight to work with. They are full of curiosity and motivation to learn everything about the world in which they live. They need a safe and stimulating environment in which to develop, and friends to share their interests.

11 Working with 5–7 Year-olds

Part of your training may be working in a school with 5–7 year-olds. Not many education authorities employ childcare workers in infant, first or lower schools, but you may be able to work in a school with this age-group as part of your training. Special schools will have children aged five, six and seven, but the children in these schools will be developmentally delayed in one or more aspects of their development, and to understand normal development you will need to be in an ordinary school.

The school day

In general, the children will be in school for a morning and an afternoon session, although some schools find it better for the younger children to start with one session only, increasing the time gradually over the dinner period until the children have settled in happily. A large school can be a frightening place for a young child, particularly for those children who have had no pre-school experience. The large, noisy playground, the vast dinner hall, and the lavatories outside the classroom will all need getting used to, and the wise head teacher understands this and will be sympathetic to the needs of the children.

Aims

Schools are all different, and may have different philosophies and aims for the children in their care. Some will lay emphasis on academic ability, others may have a reputation for music or for art. Some schools may give a great deal of pastoral care to the families, while others may feel that this is inappropriate for teachers. All schools will have to carry out the demands of the National Curriculum, which tests children's ability in many areas before they move on to junior or middle school at seven plus. Your supervisor should discuss this with you at the start of the placement.

ACTIVITY

Make a board game with the children which will help them with some aspect of mathematics. Your supervisor will tell you what area the children in class might need some extra help with. Write an observation of the children using the game, and evaluate how well it works for the age-group.

The class team

Each class will have its own teacher, with perhaps some help from untrained ancillary staff, who will mix paints, cover books and may do some art activities with the children. Your role is quite different from that of a 'helper'. You will be expected to be responsible for the health and care of the children and to aid the teacher in all areas of child development. It is important for you to realise that you will work directly to the teacher in the class, and to discuss with him or her any activities that may be planned.

You will be valued as a member of the staff team, but may need to establish your role in initiating activities and explaining in what ways these will aid children's intellectual, social, physical or emotional development. Most of the creative activities that you will carry out with the 3–5 year-olds will be relevant to the older children, but with one important difference – the children will be expected to finish any work started, and perhaps to extend it further.

You will be invaluable in adding to theme work, whether it is in the area of music, books, art, displays, or drama. Remember that whatever you do has to be fully discussed with the teacher in the class first, who may ask you to do something different from what you had planned.

Children work together in small groups

Accessible, well-organised shelving

A well-organised infant classroom

There is no reason not to help with preparing materials such as paints and, as in the nursery, part of your job will be to make sure that all the equipment is in good condition. But a good student will also want to help with children's learning, although it may take the teacher a little while to trust you with this. Your college will expect you to keep up your observations and will ask you to do some on children's reading, mathematical and scientific experiences.

ACTIVITY

1 Using clay with the children, ask them what they would like to make to add to the home corner. The ideas should come from them. When finished, allow the clay to harden. The children may then paint it, and after varnishing, the finished articles should last for some time.

2 Read a book without pictures to the children. Ask the children to draw some scenes from their imagination, and make these drawings into a book.

3 Take a small group of children shopping with you. (You may have to take another member of staff as well because, as a student, you are not insured to take children out on your own.) Having asked the children to decide what they want to cook, let them buy the correct amount of ingredients, pay for them, and make sure they have the right change. They will be able to weigh and measure everything themselves. Your role will be supervision and encouragement.

Learning through play

Although all schools vary, a good school will understand the importance of children learning through play, and through exploration. Hopefully, the children will not be told that they can 'play' when they have finished their 'work', but if this is so it is up to you to make sure the time allocated for play is used well, and the children learn from their experience. Most schools will have set times for outside play, and it might be possible to make this more rewarding for the children, by joining in their play and extending it.

ACTIVITY

Buy some grass seed with the children. Choose different mediums on which to grow the grass, such as sand, earth, blotting paper, and cardboard. Which grass grows the fastest? Which looks the healthiest? Why?

Children of this age will go on more outings than the younger age-groups. Outings provide a valuable learning experience, and you will help the children make the most of them by listening to and answering their questions, finding books and resources to enrich visits, and extending the learning later in creative art, music or drama.

Check list   **Have you:**

prepared any creative activities, and seen them completed?

read or told a story to a group of children?

led a music session, perhaps with movement as well?

shopped and cooked with the children?

taken part in theme work?

been on any outings with the children?

become involved in team discussions, contributing your own suggestions?

taken part in helping children with their reading, writing and mathematics?

kept up with your observations?

12 Working with Children with Special Needs

A number of children have needs which call for special education to be provided, either in an ordinary school with support teaching, in a special unit within an ordinary school, or in a special school. In almost all special schools, you will work as part of a team, regardless of the age of the children. The types of special need are emotional and behavioural problems, moderate learning difficulties, severe learning difficulties, speech and language difficulties, visual and hearing impairment, motor impairment, and autism.

As there are opportunities for future employment in special schools, many colleges will attempt to place their students in centres for children with special needs.

There has been a move during recent years to integrate all children into mainstream schools, and many students will have contact with children with special needs in ordinary schools.

If you have had no previous contact with a child with a special need you may be apprehensive before starting a placement at a special school, but after two or three days the vast majority of students really enjoy the work, and many decide that this is what they want to do once they are qualified.

Some common worries

Apart from a general fear of the unknown, students may be concerned about:

- how to cope with children in a group
- how to communicate with the children
- coping with incontinent children
- lifting children in a skilled way
- dealing with strange patterns of behaviour.

If you spend time observing the routine and noticing how procedures are carried out, you will quickly settle in and feel comfortable in the placement.

Teamwork in special schools

You will be working with teachers and nursery nurses, and will very quickly become a valued member of the team and be given the opportunity to use many skills. You may find yourself working closely with one child, or with very small groups of children. Children may not respond or behave in a predictable way, and there will be opportunities for you to use your own initiative. You will gradually become more competent. Any worries or negative feelings should be freely and openly discussed with your supervisor and with your personal tutor at college.

Many professional people will be in contact with the school, and may visit the school frequently, some on a daily basis. You will develop an understanding of each profession and learn how to liaise effectively with all those involved with the children and the family.

ACTIVITY————————————————

Discover the number of visiting specialists and their roles. What help does each one give the children?

Special skills

Depending on the type of school, there will be opportunities for you to gain special skills, such as learning to sign and lip read in a school for hearing-impaired children, the use of braille in a school for visually impaired children, and a knowledge of the use of computers – which may be widely used with many types of special need. These skills can be shared with the student group in college through examples and in discussion.

Communicating by sign language

Activities

Most activities carried out with 3–7 year-olds would be appropriate for use in special schools. Always discuss whatever you wish to do with the team first.

Check list

Have you:

seen the reception and departure of children?

assisted the teacher or nursery nurse in general activities throughout the day?

assisted in the preparation of play and teaching materials and the setting up of the rooms?

helped to care for the physical needs of the children, toileting, dressing and assisting at mealtimes?

participated in physical education sessions and swimming?

observed other people working with the children, such as speech therapists, occupational therapists and physiotherapists?

read stories to groups of children or to individuals, whenever appropriate?

carried out musical and craft activities with groups or individuals, as often as possible?

Rewards

One of the rewards of working with children with special needs is the very close relationship that develops between the adults and the children. There is also great pleasure in observing a child making progress in terms of communication, emotional stability, physical skills and independence.

13 Moving into Employment

A nursery nurse in her first job

A few months before the end of your training, you should start to think seriously about future employment. Some courses will offer wider employment opportunities, while other courses allow students to have immediate access to higher education. Many students start training with an idea of where they wish to work, but experience on the course may show them that they prefer one particular age-group to another, or that they find one type of placement is particularly suited to their skills, temperament and personality. Students will have different needs in seeking employment, and have different choices to make. Younger students living in rural areas will have less choice than mature students living in urban areas. There is less day-care and nursery education provision in the country, and for some the choice will be limited. Working as a nanny and living in with a family will enable the younger person to leave home and seek wider horizons.

Settling in

Settling in to new places is always challenging, but you will have done this many times during your training and will have also helped children to meet new situations. Looking back to earlier chapters where settling in has been discussed in some detail will help you to make a satisfactory start and a good first impression.

It is important to recognise that although you will not have the supervision you had as a student, a probationary period is usual before the employment is secure. It should be made clear exactly what is expected of you in the job, and to whom you should refer if there should be any problems. You will be expected to maintain professional standards, whether you are employed in the private sector as a nanny or in the public sector in education or day-care.

Most employers will understand that moving from student to fully-qualified practitioner requires support and the opportunity to discuss routines, policies, roles and the aims of the establishment or the wishes of the parent, so as to reach an understanding of what is required.

Showing enthusiasm for all aspects of the work and taking part in extra-curricular and social activities will speed up the settling-in process, and encourage others to accept you as a valuable member of the staff. It is a matter of confidence and personality as to how quickly you will feel at ease with the situation. Most college tutors are very pleased to see ex-students, and ready to discuss both triumphs and disasters.

Joining a professional association or union

College tutors may have stressed the importance of belonging to either a professional association or a trade union, and by doing so employees can gain support and security as well as the opportunity to meet others within the profession. This can be just as important for those working in families (the private sector) as for those working in the public sector.

Nannies should also make sure that they have professional indemnity insurance in case a claim of professional negligence should be made against them.

Support groups

It is a good idea to join a support group. These often advertise in the local press and in *Nursery World*. Nannies often feel as isolated as young mothers do, being on their own with small children for the whole day, and they need to share experiences and socialise with others in a similar situation. For childcare workers in the public sector, some of the larger local authorities run their own induction programmes, and these can be a tremendous support for those starting out in childcare. Discussion groups may be run in some areas, where you can obtain up-to-date information and benefit from a free exchange of views.

Possible problems

It can happen that the first choice of employment does not meet your expectations. In a private family, this could be because:

● you do not have a contract of employment
● the contract is being disregarded

- your views on child-rearing are not compatible with those of the parents
- you suffer from home-sickness or loneliness
- you dislike the family lifestyle, values and opinions
- there is a personality clash, and perhaps even harassment of some kind.

In the public sector you might be unhappy because:

- you feel you are not accepted within the team
- there is a mismatch between the job and the job description
- you have reservations about childcare practices
- there are personality clashes.

In both the public and the private sector, you may find it difficult to manage on the money you have been offered and need to change jobs for this reason. You may find that the job is not making use of all your skills, and that you are bored as a result. The journey to work may be more troublesome than you had anticipated.

All these are quite valid reasons for a change of job, but do try to resolve any difficulties if it is at all possible, as your prospects for another job will be greater if you can show that you have persevered for some time. All experience is valuable, and you will find that overcoming initial difficulties can be the best experience of all.

Career progression

Anyone in a professional job needs to think about their career path, and applying their skills, expertise and knowledge to an ever wider field. Having made a success of your first job, you will need to take stock of your achievements and think about what you have especially enjoyed. Perhaps you will feel you would like to extend your experience in one area or move on to a more challenging job.

In the past there was a shortage of in-service courses, but in 1984 the Certificate in Post-Qualifying Studies (CPQS) was developed (from 1991: Diploma in Post-Qualifying Studies). This is a course of study composed of six modules, on offer to nursery nurses with two years' post-qualifying experience. Each module takes a term at a college of further education, and you would be released from work for one day a week to attend the course. Coursework is also carried out in the workplace.

This course has been highly successful. It allows students to evaluate their practice and to consider the employment they are pursuing at the time. It can motivate students to take up new positions, such as managing nurseries, lecturing in colleges of further education on the NNEB and BTEC courses, undertaking educational welfare work, and entering early years teacher training courses, in some cases with one year's credit.

This advanced course of study has not only allowed nursery nurses to progress within their own profession, but has gone some way towards improving the image and status of nursery nurses.

Widening your horizons

Once you have gained some experience there are many jobs available to you, such as:

- Working in hospitals with sick children, possibly leading to secondment on to the Hospital Playworkers course.
- Working in hospitals in a special care baby unit, with premature and sick babies.
- Working in assessment centres, alongside a play therapist, helping to identify children with special needs. Here, the nursery nurse's skill in observation techniques is particularly valuable.
- Working first as a deputy and then in charge of day-care units. Someone who is experienced and holds the DPQS would progress faster.

There is continuous change and development of opportunities within the childcare professions, and if you are seriously thinking of furthering your career you should read a professional magazine to keep up with what is happening.

Changing direction

As most courses encompass the two main vocational areas of education and health, it is inevitable that some people will make the decision to move into early years teacher training or into the nursing profession. Others may wish to build on their work with families by completing a social work training course.

Working with children is a fulfilling and worthwhile profession. The training can be the foundation of a very satisfying professional career.